# The
# Folly
# of God

Seminar on God

and the

Human Future

David Galston, series editor

Vol. 1: *The Folly of God*, John D. Caputo

# The
# Folly
# of God

## A Theology of the Unconditional

# John D. Caputo

POLEBRIDGE PRESS
Salem, Oregon

**Library of Congress Cataloging-in-Publication Data**
Caputo, John D.
  The Folly of God : a theology of the unconditional / by John D. Caputo.
    pages cm
  Includes bibliographical references and index.
ISBN 978-1-59815-192-3
  1. Postmodernism--Religious aspects--Christianity. I. Title.
  BR115.P74C35 2016
  231--dc23

                                                              2015031857

# Contents

Introduction: The Interests of Theology ................ 1

1. God Is Not a Supreme Being ...................... 7

2. The Unconditional ............................. 19

3. Proto-Religion ................................ 35

4. How Long Will Religion Last? ................... 47

5. In Praise of Weakness ......................... 53

6. Weakening the Being of the Supreme Being .......... 65

7. A Theology of Perhaps ......................... 73

8. The Folly of the Call .......................... 83

9. Mustard Seeds Not Metaphysics: The Theopoetics
   of the Kingdom of God ........................ 93

10. Does the Kingdom of God Need God? ............. 111

Notes ....................................... 129

Bibliography ................................. 133

Index ....................................... 137

# Abbreviations

| | |
|---|---|
| 1 Cor | 1 Corinthians |
| 1 Thess | 1 Thessalonians |
| Col | Colossians |
| Eph | Ephesians |
| Matt | Matthew |
| Phil | Philippians |
| Ps(s) | Psalm(s) |
| Rev | Revelation |

# Introduction

## The Interests of Theology

At a time when Jews expect a miracle and Greeks seek enlightenment, we speak about God's Anointed *crucified*! This is an offense to Jews, nonsense to the nations; but to those who have heard God's call, both Jews and Greeks, the Anointed represents God's power and God's wisdom; because the folly of God is wiser than humans are and the weakness of God is stronger than humans are.

—1 Cor 1:22–25[1]

The real interest of theology is not in God. At the end of the day, it is in the best interests of theology not to be content with God. Theology has other interests. I will not say higher interests because what could be higher than God? God after all is the *ens supremum*, the Supreme Being, the highest being of them all. When we give glory to God we regularly add "in the highest." If we are to allow the interests of theology to be measured by who or what is highest, God comes out on top, hands down. That is a competition that prudence dictates I decline to enter. Instead, I will strike out in the opposite direction. Conceding the high ground to the other side—let's call that "high theology," theology that can have no higher interest than God—my contention is that theology has deeper interests than God. We could call the opposing tendency "deep theology" but I prefer to call it "radical theology," meaning getting down in the dirt and digging down into the roots of theology.

I also contend that because high theology is too often high and mighty it is well described as "strong theology," and that strong theology has been too strong for its own good. So my general line

1

of argument is that the best interests of theology would be served were it not so high and mighty. The cause to which I regularly contribute, by contrast, is of a more modest and timid sort. This I call "weak theology," in keeping with what St. Paul calls the "weakness of God" (1 Cor 1:25) where weak theologians are markedly afraid of heights and of being too puffed up, not only by knowledge but also by power. So when it comes to God and theology, to thinking about God, let us get our bearings right from the start: where there is height, I head for the depths; where there is a show of strength, I prefer weakness. Instead of high and mighty, we radical theologians seek the deep and weak! If we want to change theology—or anything else—change the metaphors.

In what follows I first address my fear of heights (chapters 1–4). I start with a religiously salutary and genuinely theological atheism—about God in the highest—which I treat not as the end of theology but the beginning (chapter 1). I then unearth the depth dimension that is sought in radical theology in terms of the "unconditional," which I propose, entirely conscious of the paradox, is the only condition under which we can think through what is really going on in theology. To speak of a theology of the unconditional, as I do here, is for me a felicitous tautology; once you say the one you say the other and you are repeating yourself, happily, because it bears repetition (chapter 2). That leads me to propose what I call a certain proto-religion, or religionless religion, or religion without religion, which turns on a deeper resonance with the unconditional in our lives, which subtends the furious and futile debate between theism and atheism, or religion and secularism, going on up above (chapter 3). I conclude this leg of the argument—about the depth of the unconditional—by asking, given the increasing incredulity with which garden variety religion is greeted, how much longer will religion last? (chapter 4).

As my advocacy of weakness, which belongs no less to my idea of a theology of the unconditional, requires no less an explanation, I then take up the logic, if it is a logic, of weakening (chapters 5–9).

First, I explain what perversity made me take the side of weakness instead of strength in order to speak of God, who is quite famous for being omnipotent (chapter 5). That allows me to get to what the "weakness of God" really means and why this figure, which is not of my devising—it comes from First Corinthians!—has so strong a hold on me (chapter 6). That in turn allows me to introduce another perverse proposal: to approach God not as a necessary being, as in classical theology, but in the more radical terms of the may-being of a divine "perhaps" (chapter 7). That brings me to a crucially important point in my argument, upon which everything before and afterwards depends in my theology of the unconditional, the dynamics of "call" and "response" (chapter 8). I then take up the final implication of the logic of weakening, that the weakness of God requires in turn a corresponding weakening of theology itself as a form of discourse. To this end I turn to the kingdom of God, the coming of which was announced by Jesus, which, I contend, is to be addressed not in a bombastic theology of omnipotence but in the softer, lower, and more dulcet tones of what I call a theopoetics (chapter 9). This could not be more important, because the kingdom of God, after all, is not a particular case in point in Christianity; it is the whole point.

In the concluding section (chapter 10), I will bring the entire analysis to head, or maybe better back down to earth, by addressing head-on a question I have brought down on myself. As I have no wish to disagree with Jesus, the problem I have is very considerable. Assuming that the argument I have made on behalf of the theology of the unconditional holds up, how can the rule of God—*basileia, regnum, imperium*—be carried out without a high and mighty God to do the ruling? Is that not the heights, or the depths, of folly? Or might the opposite be the case: that if the High and Mighty One ever showed up, everything in the kingdom of God would be ruined? To put it rather pointedly, does the kingdom of God need God? Or might the opposite be the case, that God needs the kingdom of God? (chapter 10)

Throughout I will not deny that the unconditional is risky business. It is not an investment that guarantees a good return. That is
why I am presenting this little book on a theology of the unconditional in and under the name of the "folly of God" (*to moron tou
theou*), which will have been my third try at tracing the logic (*logos*)
of the cross outlined by Paul in 1 Corinthians 1.[2] Having thereby
completed a trilogy I did not set out to write, it is beginning to
look like there is a method to my madness. If so, it is because I have
adopted the method of madness itself, the logic of a fool's logic
(*morologia*), remembering that in French *folie* also means madness.
To put it in a way calculated to scandalize, this is a study of God's
own madness, God's own foolishness. God? How mad! What folly!
That is what I propose, or rather what I propose about what Paul
is proposing.

In saying all this, of course, I am trying to get your attention. I
am not coming out against wisdom, sanity, and strength in any and
every sense. That would be simply mad, and I am saying that nothing is simple, even madness and folly. I have in mind to isolate the
method of a certain divine madness, one that follows along (*meta*)
the way (*odos*) of the cross by mining the depths of Paul's explosive
language about the "weakness of God" and the "folly of God" and
about the way God sides with "non-being" over being, all language
calculated to get the attention of the Greek philosophers at Corinth,
which I am sure left them lost for words.

But I insist that this language cannot be used as a ruse, a power
play, a strategy, a bait and switch game. It must not turn out, at the
end of the day, that it is God on high who has the real power after
all and God who outsmarts his enemies down below. That is the old
high and mighty theology, not the theology of the unconditional.
That would just make God a kind of heavenly hustler from on high.
It would enter God into the games of power and wisdom as they
are played out in the world, God lying low in order to come from
on high later on when the other side least expects it. That is precisely the treachery and resentment of which Christianity is accused

by Friedrich Nietzsche (1844–1900), the ruse of making weakness
a weapon to lay low the strong and thereby win the day. Then it
would turn out that the theology of the cross is a good investment,
a clever disguise worn by the theology of glory, and the folly of God
would just be a way to fool the world.

By taking a stand with the unconditional, I am proposing instead
to follow the way of weakness and non-being all the way to the end.
My claim is that a theology of the unconditional is where a theology
of the cross leads; it is the way to follow the way of the cross. When
we run into the heroes of the unconditional, the right religious
and theological reaction is, What folly! *Quelle folie!* How mad! The
line between a fool and a hero has always been notoriously thin.
The wager behind a theology of the unconditional is that there is
another strength and wisdom lodged *within* weakness and folly, one
that the street smart world will treat with scorn. I am proposing a
double folly, both God's and ours, which means I propose both
God and theology *crucified!* To the pious, who prefer their God to
come on high and lay low their enemies with miracles and magic,
I propose a scandal, and to the classical theologians, who prefer
a theology that provides proofs and propositions about a Hyper
Being with Super-Powers aplenty, I propose a fool's logic, *theologia*
as *morologia*, the foolish nonsense (*moria*) of the unconditional. A
crucified God and a crucified theology, both left humbled, hanging
naked and deprived of glory—but, once again, all this in the service
not of simple death and destruction but of life, just as resurrection
follows crucifixion. That is our challenge.

The trick will be not to compromise the cross by turning weakness, folly, and non-being into cunning stratagems, making them
into long-term investments in an economy of salvation in which
God and theology turn out to be the winners. The unconditional
is not a winning strategy and theology is not about winning. That
would be docetic, the one heresy, I am proud to say, I really do
renounce. For then the weakness, non-being and folly, the nails and
wood of the cross, would be merely apparent, God freely holding

one hand behind the divine back, an *incognito* under which the theology of glory is getting ready to spring its trap. That would just be clever, just plain street smart, smart as the world knows smart, God outsmarting the world. That is not the unconditional. That is not the folly of God I am defending here, where the strength is lodged in the very heart of the weakness, where the wisdom is found deep in the heart of the folly. The *skandalon* and the *moria* is that we may not win at all.

# 1

# God Is Not
# a Supreme Being

## The Supreme Being

In preferring to go deeper and to give up going higher, I am, to begin with, simply updating theology by reversing the ancients' attitudinal preference for "up," which reflects a pre-Copernican turn of mind and an ancient sense of orientation. For example, suppose the right wing's "rapture" were to come about (and I for one would not be downcast to see them go so long as I am left behind), and the chosen all around the globe were all lifted straight "up" to heaven "above," all at the same time. Then they would all head out in different directions, so that not only would those of us left behind never see them again, but they would never see one another again. They would be caught up in a final inter-stellar scattering, racing away from one another at an ever accelerating rate, which is not exactly the last round-up they seem to have in mind. So the time has long since come to reexamine how to orient oneself in space, including and especially cosmo-theological space. The time has come to remodel and re-imagine theology in accord with a more up-to-date sense of cosmological direction.[3] Accordingly, I hope to show that as a mode of thinking and inquiring in what has come to be known as the postmodern world, the best interests of theology are to be found deep down in the depths of our experience. Thus as a way of coping with the enormous authority that God in the highest has accumulated over several millennia now, as a way of dodging its almost overwhelming power and prestige,

7

not to mention syncing with contemporary astro-physics, I reverse
the image and invoke the opposite measuring rod. I insist that everything in theology is to be measured by depth, not height. The
best interests of theology lie not in God in the highest but in the
depths of God, something deep within God, even older than God,
or deeper than God, and for that very same reason, deep within us,
we and God always being intertwined.

This means that if someone maintains, as just about everyone
in the mainstream theistic traditions maintains, that God is the
Supreme Being, the highest being, then the proper theological
response is to deny it. As my favorite theologian Paul Tillich put
it, the concept of the "existence of God"—of the highest entity
or existent, as an identifiable somebody or something—is "half-
blasphemous and mythological." It is something like the ancients
treating thunder as a god, or the sun, or nowadays imagining a
global rapture. This text is of some importance to me as it provides
the thread that runs throughout this book, in which I seek to follow
it to its ultimate conclusion:

> God is no object for us as subjects. He [sic—it was 1946] is
> always that which precedes this division. But, on the other
> hand, we speak about him and we act upon him, and we can-
> not avoid it, because everything which becomes real to us
> enters the subject-object correlation. Out of this paradoxical
> situation the half-blasphemous and mythological concept of
> the "existence of God" has arisen. And so have the abortive
> attempts to prove the existence of this "object." To such a
> concept and to such attempts atheism is the right religious and
> theological reply.[4]

To turn the business of theology over to proving the existence
of a Supreme Being and to working out his—or hers or its (we see
at once the terrible problem with pronouns that high theology
then inherits)—properties or names; and then to work out the very
complex relations that a Supreme Being such as this has with all the

other beings, not just on earth but in our solar system or in the universe or in all the possible universes (that little thumbnail sketch of the history of astrophysics gives us an idea of another, increasingly pressing set of insuperable problems); to turn theology into all that, Tillich is saying, is not in the best interests of theology. Indeed it is the height of irreligion, of something "half-blasphemous and mythological," a phrase I will often have occasion to repeat. Consider how the simple grammatical shift of putting Heaven in the plural, switching from Heaven to the heavens, can throw high theology into so much confusion. Where, in Heaven's name, are we to pass our afterlife? "Up" in "Heaven"? "Out" on some distant galaxy, far, far away? Surely, the time has come for theology to come up with a new grammar, new directions and a new sense of orientation, a new theo-global positioning system. The Supreme Being causes supreme problems, insuperable ones, the result of which too often seems to turn the debates of theology into a sophisticated and complicated argument about how best to howl at the moon (or the sky!). The more supreme the entity, the more insuperable the problem. It is in the best of interests of theology to avoid it.

The solution that Tillich strikes is simple, swift, sweeping, shocking, and decisive: atheism. Striking a contrarian atheistic position like that seems downright ornery and short-sighted for a theologian, even foolish. By denying that God exists, theology gives every appearance of biting the hand that has fed it for millennia. But this is not just any atheism. Notice that Tillich says that atheism is the best "religious and theological" response to such an idea of God. This atheism is of a uniquely religious and theological provenance and purpose. Tillich was a theologian, a very prominent one, one of the most famous theologians of the twentieth century. Tillich was not recommending that theology should be dropped from the curriculum on the grounds that its subject matter does not exist. He was a professor of theology at Union Theological Seminary, Harvard University and the University of Chicago, so we may assume that, while there might be a touch of divine folly in what he was saying, he was not foolishly trying to put theology professors out of a job. That would not have been in the best interest of theology or of Professor Tillich, who, like everyone else, was trying to earn a living.

In saying that the real interests of theology lie elsewhere, he was thinking of its own best interests, and those of theology as a discipline, as a mode of serious, honest inquiry in the contemporary world, as a mode of what I am calling radical theology. Where Tillich would have spoken of getting in step with the "modern" world, seventy-five years later I would say "postmodern," and seventy-five years from now they will be calling it something else, who knows what or post-what. Whatever we call it, the future of theology lies in getting past this idea of God as the highest being and, since we cannot get higher, since classical "high" theology claims the high ground, the very highest, we have to dig deeper, down to the roots. Radical theology starts by bidding adieu to God, *adieu à Dieu*, as the *ens supremum*. It starts out by weakening the God of high and mighty theology. Or rather, since that looks like a show of hubris and subjective strength on our part, let us say not that we are weakening anything, but that we are letting the Supreme Being of strong theology weaken into something more truly God-like. Think of it as letting the over-tensed muscles of strong theology relax into a more natural look, letting it strike a more suitably theological, more deeply or properly religious bearing, more amicable and humane. We are letting God escape the grip of the mythology and half-blasphemy of a Big Being in the sky—for the sake of God. This is not our doing, but God's; we are simply reporters embedded at the scene of theology.

## Theology Begins with Atheism

So we start this little book with a bit of folly, with a paradox: that it is in the best interests of theology to say that God does not exist; that the real interest of theology is not in God; that what is needed to get theology going, to get it in gear, is atheism. But remember, for Tillich atheism is not the end of theology but the beginning. Theology begins with atheism, a theological atheism not to be confused with garden variety atheism, which suffers from the same confusion as theism. Garden variety theists and atheists are both arguing about whether there is or there is not a Supreme Being. Tillich would have had absolutely no time for the time that is being wasted by the "new atheists"[5] in disproving the existence of this God. They attempt to disprove the existence of the same half-blasphemous and mythological concept of God as the theologians are bending their efforts to prove. The atheists are trying to break down a door that is already wide open in radical theology, so if you lead a charge like that you will end up flat on your face. The debate between the theists and the atheists is futile. It proves nothing because they are arguing about nothing, literally. Tillich's claim is that there is nothing there; there is no "there" there, no Supreme Being to prove or disprove. That is not what interests theology, not where its interests lie.

Nor do we make any headway by concluding that the whole contest ends in a draw, that we must suspend judgment, and that the only safe and reasonable position on the matter is agnosticism. Agnosticism is as badly misled as theism and atheism, since in withholding judgment about the existence of this mythological and half-blasphemous being the agnostic makes the same presupposition, that the thing about which we should withhold judgment is the Supreme Being. The agnostic assumes that this is a legitimate question to which we just do not know the answer. But it is not a legitimate question; it is a mistaken one. The question needs to be questioned, pulled up root and branch by radical theology, undermined, dug under, subverted, displaced, gotten around, put out of action. Here is a case where yes, no, or maybe do not exhaust all the options. I do not want to be violent.

By expelling this question—a bad and ancient theological habit!—I am not trying to discourage freedom of thought. On the contrary, as thinkers, we reserve the right to ask every question, but not every question is a good question. The best response to some questions is not to answer them but to question the question—like whether such a Supreme Being exists or not. That is like forcing an answer to the question: Have you stopped cheating on your taxes—no straddling the fence, yes or no? Theology, the interests of theology, the best interests of theology depend on undermining this question by undermining its subject matter. The depths of theology, radical theology, theology as deep thinking, and possibly—I do not want to sound chauvinistic or provincial—as the very deepest thinking of all, depend on it. Contrary to Martin Heidegger (1889–1976), theology thinks and questions, and it thinks and questions deeply, reaching down into the depths of our lives and bleeding into everything we do, all of our beliefs and practices, every last one. That's how much depends on getting this right.

That Tillich is describing a theologically sensitive atheism becomes clear from the fact that he immediately adds that an atheism like this is well known among all the mystics. Meister Eckhart, one of the greatest mystics, said—and this is one of the most famous of his sayings—that he prays to God to rid him of God, to make him free of God.[6] That is a memorable formulation of a mystical atheism and of radical theology. I do not know how it can be improved upon. Eckhart perfectly encapsulates a kind of mystical folly and a paradox worthy to be pondered, revisited daily, and held (deeply, of course) in our hearts. Some of the very best things ever said about God are said by mystics who say that of God we cannot say a thing. In saying this I am not trying to be clever. Well, even if I am, I am pointing to the profound resources of the mystical tradition which has learned how to not speak by speaking, to advance while erasing its own tracks, to twist and turn language so as to expose the ruptures and omissions and distortions that inhere in everything we say when we approach matters so deep. The mystics are the most profound of God's fools.

The God Eckhart is trying to free us from is a God of our own construction, a God cut to fit the size of our images and concepts, propositions and arguments, not just the God of the philosophers but also the God of the theologians, of anything and everything we think we can say of God. But getting rid of that God does not spell the simple end of God for Eckhart, but the beginning, the genuine entry or breakthrough into the depths of God—the God *to whom* he is *praying*, let us say the God beyond God, the God without God. Here again caution is required lest we confuse "beyond" with "above" and fall into the old trap of the *ens supremum*, of God as the being in the highest.[7] On the contrary, this God is the "ground" of God and it is found not up above, but down in the "ground" of soul, which is the Augustinian style of approaching God that Tillich advances, where God is lodged deep in our hearts or minds, in what Augustine calls our *memoria*. We must be vigilant about the lure of high theology and not allow ourselves to imagine a God dwelling high up in the sky, in a height beyond all heights, so high that we simply lack the thrust to launch a name that would fly that high, so high that we cannot speak a word that would carry that far up. Think down, not up; think deep, not high.

What we learn from the mystics, Tillich says, is that God is the "Unconditional" (or sometimes the "Unconditioned")[8] and that we cannot "fix" God as an "object," as an identifiable thing that we as thinking "subjects" can pick out and identify, or reverse wise as an identifiable subject who can pick out us as objects.[9] The whole subject/object framing imposes a set of conditions and has to go. It keeps us stuck in the wrong dimension and makes us miss the depth dimension. God, *what is going on in the name of God* (this expression is important for me and I will keep coming back to it), does not work like that. But it is not only the mystics who warn us against thinking of God like this, Tillich says. We learn the same lesson from itchy and annoying philosophers like Socrates, whom the Athenians charged with atheism because he said that celestial objects like the sun and the moon are not gods. Actually, Socrates was guilty as charged: to such a concept of God the right religious theological reply *is* atheism. Furthermore, the Jews were charged with being atheists by the nations (gentiles) since the Jews were atheists about the gods of the nations, even as the early Christians were considered atheists by those who adhered to the "powers and principalities" (Eph 6:11–13, the devil and his minions), about which the Christians were indeed atheists. We do not deal with the powers and principalities, Tillich is saying, by thinking of God as a higher opposing power or counter-principality—that is the mythological God he is criticizing.

## Ground of Being

Tillich is worried about "the inadequacy of all limiting names," about anything that would limit God, confine God, make God into something finite or definite, limited or delimited, because God is infinite and unlimited. Finite things come to be and pass away, but God is infinite and everlasting. God is that from which finite things arise and into which they return, and so God is the inexhaustible "womb" of all things, to employ a more feminine and less patriarchal figure. To say that God exists is to say that God is a definite entity, supreme but definite, and if definite, then finite. But God is not a finite, definite being because God is the (indefinite, indefinable) ground of definite beings, that from which they emerge and into which they return. Just so, God is not an "object" for our minds, not a particular thing we can pick out, but the very light in which objects are visible and by which eyes can see, which is a more Platonic and Augustinian way to approach God. God is not a "cause" of which the things that happen in the world are "effects" but the light in which the distinction between cause and effect is drawn.

It is half-blasphemous and mythological to think of God as a mover who moves things (the first or "prime mover," of course), or the agent who does things, the "first cause" of all things. God is instead the infinite and inexhaustible ground in which all such distinctions and processes take place, in which all things have their being. God is not something or someone (neither he nor she nor it) doing something, like causing or making or even choosing to be the ground, nor in a more hands-off way supervising their production from afar and directing it wisely to an end. God is not a highest being but the very being of beings, or the ground of beings, the light of beings, the "deep," boundless, ceaseless, illimitable, unrestricted resource of anything and everything, of every word or distinction between words that we utter. That means that everything we say about God is "symbolic," since everything we say is drawn from finite beings, the only ones with which we are familiar, of which God is the illimitable light and source.

We should resist concluding at this point, as we might well be tempted, that Tillich is thus a "pantheist," that his atheism criticizes theism in the name of pantheism. He is not saying that God is anything and everything but that God is the ground of anything and everything. Just as God is not any *one* being or thing, neither is God the sum total of all beings or things. Just as God is not one finite entity, God is not all finite entities bundled together. God is their ground, their source and resource, the spring from which they all spring forth and into which they all fall back, not as effects from a cause but as things emergent from a ground. The ground is not one thing or all things. The best way to put this is to call it, not pantheism, but pan*en*theism, and to say not that God is all or all is God, but that God is *in* all things and all things are *in* God. Pantheism, on the other hand, is a very strange position and I doubt any philosopher or theologian has ever actually held it. It would claim that this computer on which I am typing is God, that my annoying in-laws are a family of Gods, that the old car I just traded in is God, that the high school I attended years ago is God, and so on. I have never met anyone, in the flesh or in the library, who actually held such a view.

God is the ground of being, or as he also says being-itself (*ipsum esse*), not a particular existing being (*ens*). But there is one other possibility to which Tillich gives short shrift, and ironically it is the position of Thomas Aquinas (Thomistic), the very one which the more Augustinian-minded Tillich is using to illustrate the short-

sighted theology of the *ens supremum*. Tillich does not seem to have
noticed the explosion of Thomistic studies going on around him
in those days.[10] He does not reckon with the fact that Aquinas was
acutely conscious of the problem of saying that if God exists, if God
is an existing being (*ens*), we would be in danger of making God
finite. As virtually all the mid-twentieth century commentators were
pointing out, Aquinas said that, in addition to calling God the first
being (*ens primum*)—he did not forbid it, piety among other things
demands it—we should also say, still more rigorously (*proprie*), that
God is being itself (*ipsum esse*). Then Aquinas agrees with Tillich?
Not exactly, because Aquinas adds what Tillich wants to subtract,
that God is *ipsum esse subsistens*, "subsistent" (existent) being itself
(both *esse* and *ens*). Aquinas means that God is being itself subsisting or existing as an independent reality in and through itself (*per se
subsistens*), such that if all creatures disappeared God would still be
left standing. Although Aquinas was famous for his Aristotelianism,
this was a remarkably Platonic position to strike. Plato held that
there is a form of tree-ness itself, subsisting or existing in itself, in
which individual existing trees participate in order to be trees. Aquinas said that, while the Platonists are wrong when it comes to trees
and other finite essences, what they are saying happens to be true of
God. God is being itself, subsisting through itself, in which created
beings participate in order to be at all. The considerable greatness
of Aquinas as a metaphysical theologian lay in the impressive way
he worked this out.

By making this very Platonic gesture, Aquinas has cut off in
advance, by some seven centuries, half of Tillich's objection (the
half-blasphemous half) about limiting God, making God a finite
entity, but not the other half, Tillich's other ("mythological")
objection. For Aquinas treats God as an agent who does things or
makes things, a person who makes decisions, a mover who chooses
to move things (the first or "prime mover," of course), the "first
cause" of all things. Aquinas insists all such language is proper
but analogical. But for Tillich it is weaker than that, not proper

but metaphorical, and the failure to acknowledge that is precisely "mythological." I think that Tillich gets it right when he says that speaking of God like this, *as if* God were a personal agent, personifying God, is an unavoidable but "symbolic" way to talk about what is deepest in our lives and in reality. The mythological sets in when we literalize the symbolic, when we forget that the symbol is a symbol. I would tweak this only slightly and say that it is a "poetic" way of treating God. I think saying that God and high theology are to be understood as *poems* will solve a lot of problems. But that will require a separate discussion that I will take up below, when I propose the best interests of theology are served if theology recognizes that it is in fact, more properly speaking, a "theopoetics," and ultimately, at the end of the day, a theopoetics of the kingdom of God (chapter 9). That will supply the final piece of the puzzle that will allow us to ask—and I admit this sounds like a foolish question—does the kingdom of God need God? If you are wanting in poetic soul you have no business wanting to do theology.

For Tillich to treat God as an agent would be to compromise what Tillich means when he says that God is the "unconditional," which is a central point that needs to be clarified.

# 2

# The Unconditional

The real interest of theology is not in God but in the unconditional. The sustained attempt to think the unconditional, to raise the question as such, is called radical theology, which takes up the question of God because God is one of the first things we think of when we think of something unconditional. If we wish to think at all, we have to think of something unconditional. To do so, we may or may not think of God; it depends on what we mean by "God." Even better, it depends upon what we mean by "we." So we—who have grown up with the name of God rattling around in our heads—start with God. But we radical theologians do not stop with God. It is in the best interests of theology to keep on thinking, to think God through, to think through God, all the way down to the roots, down to what Meister Eckhart called the ground of God, the depths of God. As a terminological matter, to keep things straight, Eckhart called this ground the "Godhead" of God, or the God-ness of God, the dark region from which God has emerged, like a wave tossed up by the sea (the "deep"). The Godhead is the inexhaustible depths of God lodged beneath everything we say of God up on the surface of our discourse (in theology, philosophy, art, and piety). The real interest of theology is in something deeper than God, deep within God, and deep within ourselves, something older and deeper than the debates that rage up above about believing and not believing in God, in the existence or non-existence of a Supreme Being. The unconditional literally means what has been removed from all limiting conditions. The only *condition* under which we can speak of God for Tillich is to recognize that God is *unconditional*, that which

19

exceeds any condition we may impose on God, like treating God as a Supreme Being. That kind of excess (beyond conditions) is built right into what we mean by God. High theology is swept up by God in the highest; radical theology is sunk deep in the unconditional, which is older than God in the highest.

In speaking of the unconditional, we should remember that Tillich is worried about "the inadequacy of all limiting names," about anything that would limit, confine, or define the infinite and unlimited being of God. He is looking for the least limiting thing we can say about God. Of course, we must recognize that anything we say is inevitably conditioned by the language in which we say it, language being itself a condition. That in turn suggests that there might be languages in which we do not find a good equivalent to what "we" are calling God or to this distinction between conditional and unconditional. There are resonances of the unconditional in St. Anselm's famous proposal that God is that than which nothing greater can be conceived. This has traditionally been treated as an argument for the existence of God, as a way to demonstrate the existence of the *ens supremum*, the God high in the sky. As an historical matter, we should remember that Anselm proposed this reflection in the context of a prayer, so that the "argument" for Anselm presupposes the God to whom Anselm is praying.[11] So Tillich thinks that reducing this meditation to an argument is both conceptually and historically a distortion. It is certainly a conceptual black hole. The theologians and philosophers who pursue the complexities of what came to be known as the "ontological argument" (briefly: if God didn't exist, all the finite things that do exist would be greater than God) are sucked in by the gravity of a conundrum from which they never again emerge. Fond though we may be of dark depths, we radical theologians (along with not a few strong theologians like Karl Barth, Hans Urs von Balthasar, and Jean-Luc Marion!)[12] cut a wide swath around the gravitational pull of the ontological argument—and of treating Anselm's *Proslogion* as proposing one in any straightforward sense.

Following Tillich's lead, we radical theologians stick to our guns and say that Anselm has come up with something else, a wonderfully paradoxical, almost outright foolish way to say that the only condition under which we can speak of God is to say that God is the unconditional. The proper concept of God is the concept of that which exceeds any concept. The concept of the inconceivable reminds us of the "container of the uncontainable" (*khora tou akhoratou*), which is the way that Mary, the Mother of God, is depicted in the Orthodox tradition. If we say that God is this, that, or the other thing, we can be sure that we are wrong and that God exceeds any such thing as we might say. God has already left every scene we imagine before we arrive, evaded the grasp of every conceptual (from the Latin *capere*, to seize) scheme before we have conceived it. God eludes every net (condition) before we have laid it down. The concept of the inconceivable is not a way to discourage further thought about God, but a reminder that there is something fishy about the idea of God as a first being, supreme and high in the sky. All we can say is that something is going on in and under the name (of) "God," something deep down in God, something that gives us no rest, that drives us on, and that that is where the true interests of theology lie. Something deeper is urging us to think beyond the limits of what we have thought and imagined so far. Something is pushing us past the limits, telling us to go where we cannot go, to do what cannot be done, to desire with a desire beyond desire—and so forth. This very expression "and so forth" means that the process just goes on and on, but always deeper and deeper, not higher and higher!

## Joining Forces with Deconstruction

At this point I want to advance the cause of Tillich's theology by having Tillich join forces with what is called in contemporary theory "deconstruction." This is the style of thinking launched by Jacques Derrida (1930–2004) and the approach I take to theology and to

God (and to other things as well, from ethics and politics to shopping at the supermarket!). Everything I say in this little book (about a very big topic) depends on this move. This is the point where I come clean about what is commonly called my "methodology." I put this word in scare quotes because it should scare us, and that is because methods impose conditions on their subject matter. My only method is to follow along the way of the cross, like a blind man poking with a stick. So how can there be a method of discussing the unconditional? Under what methodological conditions can we discuss the unconditional? This is the sort of conundrum we regularly run up against in this field and why I admire the adroit and deft somersaults of the mystics who know how to make their way in this topsy-turvy world. Radical theology has an "apophatic" quality to it, a word we translated as "negation" or "denial" but that literally means speaking (*phasis*) in such a way as to speak away from (*apo*) or push away what you just said. If you're up on the classics, that may remind you of the story of ancient Hermes erasing his tracks after stealing Apollo's cattle, which is an exquisite image for "hermeneutics," the theory of interpretation, which is named after Hermes' stealthy ways. Apophatic means saying something while taking back what you said, erasing the traces of what you say as you say it. It is a rhetorical trope, a very handy one that you can also use to your advantage, as when you say, "modesty prevents me from claiming credit for this fortunate turn of events," which of course you just did by saying you did not. So I agree to say that deconstruction is my methodology only under protest.

I have long been arguing that deconstruction is not bad news, that in fact it is of singular service to the "good news."[13] Deconstruction is not, as its critics have claimed, an anything-goes relativism, but a way to think the unconditional, and so it is of singular value to theology, especially to a radical theology in the tradition launched by Tillich, which I am calling a theology of the unconditional. In deconstruction, the unconditional is thought out in terms of what Derrida calls the "undeconstructible." I hasten to add that Derrida is a secular thinker who "quite rightly passes for an atheist,"[14] and certainly not a theologian. That is telling from Tillich's point of view because for Tillich the unconditional is so elementary a notion that he predicts it should show up everywhere— everywhere, that is, where we are thinking deeply or where we are making or doing or going about things in search of their depth dimension. Sure enough, there it is, as big as life, right in the core of a so-called "secular" and "atheistic" philosophy like deconstruction. That makes us worry about the much-vaunted distinction between theology and philosophy, or the religious and the secular, or faith and reason—or so it should. Derrida and Tillich, who both like to transgress or steal across borders (Hermes again!), think we should be very worried over such distinctions. Distinctions draw conditional lines in the sands of the unconditional. They draw regional boundaries in yet to be explored terrains that we should resist and distrust—to the point, I am tempted to say, of consigning them to the flames, were that not such a classical resource of strong theology! So let's turn now to deconstruction, and then come back to Tillich, God and theology.

In deconstruction, everything proceeds from the dual premise that:

1. All of our beliefs and practices, institutions and traditions, arts and sciences, all the bells and whistles as well as the basic equipment of culture, are constructions.
2. Whatever has been constructed is deconstructible—in just the way that Aristotle said that whatever comes to be also passes away—so that, if anything is not deconstructible that is only because it has not been constructed yet.

To say things are constructed is to say they are formed or forged— a word with a wonderful ambiguity, meaning both shaped and fake—in space and time. That does not mean a construction is not real; it just means that its reality is made, not found. Houses are constructed, but that does not mean they are not real. The stories told in a novel (a fiction) are made; real-life stories are made by real living forces. In the language of Edmund Husserl's (1859–1938) phenomenology,[15] we could say that constructions are "constituted"; if so, then they are not constituted by what Husserl calls transcendental consciousness but in and by a more anonymous, pre-personal, quasi-transcendental field, a complex web of interweaving forces that are linguistic, historical, social, political, gendered, bodily—"and so forth," meaning, who knows what else. Together these forces make up so many matrices—which in the shorthand notation proposed by Derrida is famously called *différance*—which produce relatively stable effects or unities of meaning. But if they are relatively stable, then they are also relatively *un*stable—and so deconstructible. You can probably see where there is leading: Tillich and Derrida and most postmodern thinkers nowadays will insist that religion is deconstructible, which theologians recognize by saying that we should not confuse religion with God, and that "God" too is deconstructible, all in the name of the unconditional. To get this straight, we have to ask what the difference is between the deconstructible and the undeconstructible.[16]

## The Deconstructible

To be deconstructible means to be reformable or transformable, which is to use the language of form (*morphe*) that goes back to Aristotle and is favored by Catherine Malabou (1959–), to my mind the most important of the new generation of French philosophers. Malabou is a former student of Derrida who has reworked the notion of deconstructibility into what she calls the "plasticity" of forms, a term also important in brain science, in which she is no less interested.[17] To be deconstructible means to be inventible, re-inventible, and even (up to a point) preventable, which is of course the language of the "event" employed by Derrida. While Malabou wants to make difference a function of changing forms, Derrida wants to make form an effect of *différance*. For Derrida any relatively stable form or meaning or structure is a unity that is formed or forged in the play of differences. A deconstruction, I hasten to add, does not mean a simple destruction, although nothing says that things that are deconstructible—and what is not?—will not someday be destroyed, whether we use the language of event or of form.

The expression "creative destruction" is not necessarily a bad way to define deconstruction, but I refuse to use it since it is one of the ways "capitalism" is defined, and there are other ethico-political things about deconstruction (its focal interest in the wholly other, *tout autre*) that make it sharply critical of the effects which capitalism is capable of producing. Capitalism tends to be creative of wealth for the wealthy and destructive of wealth for the poor, and so capitalism is less a model for deconstruction than a subject of deconstruction, that is, something badly in need of deconstruction. Deconstruction, I maintain, has more to do with the kingdom of God than capitalism; it stands on the side of the victims of capitalism (chapter 5).

In saying that a construction is a relatively stable formation, a relatively stable unity, I am saying that meaning, form, and unity are not first but last, not a priori but a posteriori. In deconstruction, diversity is not the effect of dividing a unity, but unity is an effect produced by the play of differences. Unities are derived effects and their origin is non-unitary and in that sense non-originary according to the classical model of origin, which is always one or simple. A meaning, a belief, a practice, an institution is an effect of the systems that produce meanings, beliefs, practices, and institutions. That is why a word—even a word like "God"—a work of art, or an institution (like religion) do not have a meaning but a history of ever shifting meanings. To speak of a meaning in the singular is to speak of a freeze frame, like a frozen waterfall or a "still" in a motion picture, even as a deconstruction can be carried out by writing a meticulous history which tries not to be beguiled by any particular stage in the history. A deconstruction is thus a destabilization, for better or for worse, since nothing says that this will result in an improvement instead of a disaster. The deconstructibility of any construction means that by being exposed to its future, any given construction is exposed to both a promise and a threat.

A deconstruction is not only or even primarily something that *we* are doing (given its emphasis on these systemic matrices, deconstruction is very wary of the individual "subject" or the "autonomous ego"). A deconstruction is happening whether we like or not. It is going on in the things themselves inasmuch as these things are subject to the vagaries of time over which we have no control. That is what Derrida calls an "auto-deconstruction." Nevertheless, there are deconstructive processes in which we *do* have a hand, in which we *can* participate, which means that we can try either to promote or prevent the event. In virtue of its unforeseeability, we cannot make an event happen, but we can provide the conditions under which events can happen. We can maintain ourselves in varying states of openness to the coming of what we cannot see coming. Or we can try to prevent the event. This is usually the aim of the powers that be who think the present order serves them well. But not always, as there are events we really do want to prevent because some events are disasters. But even here, Derrida says, we would do so in the name of keeping the future open, which is what ultimately matters in deconstruction. We can set up systems in which everything is monitored, controlled, kept under surveillance and the rule of law in order to prevent anything unforeseeable from happening, at least as far as that is possible. Trying to prevent the event is a conservative impulse, which is prone to become reactive, reactionary, and regressive. Trying to promote the event is pro-active and progressive, but it must take care not to become some kind of reckless, anything goes anarchy.

This debate about how rigorously the rule of law obtains is the oldest and defining debate in what is called "post-structuralism"—a more exact phrase than the more popular but elusive term "postmodernism," which refers to contemporary culture at large. The

Structuralists argued that a system like language (and "culture" at large) is ruled by a deep grammar (structures), which runs beneath the variations in the rules of grammar in the natural languages. These structures see to it that everything that happens in language is governed by a rule, or "programmed," literally written in advance. This deeper grammar was called *langue* (let's say the structure of language), as opposed to individual empirical utterances, which were called *parole*, or "events" (let's say speech acts), which occur under the rule of these laws. The Post-Structuralists—the "Sixty-eighters" (*les Soixante-huitaires*), as in 1968—resisted this and argued for a more unruly unprogrammability, a good example of which is a metaphor—putting an optimal pressure on the rules in order to produce a novel and unpredictable effect—which is what they meant by "events." Derrida produced the central document in this debate, which was very appropriately entitled *Of Grammatology*, meaning that the *logos* of *gramme* (trace) is an open-ended *logos* not a closed one, not a *pro-gramme*.[18] So Derrida was defending a theory of reason (*logos, ratio*), which is neither rationalistic, that is, where everything is contained by rules, nor irrationalistic, where there are no rules at all and anything goes. When later on Derrida wrote an essay entitled "Faith and Knowledge: The Two Sources of 'Religion' at the Limits of Reason Alone,"[19] his idea of reason was not a Kantian one, where reason encloses religion within its transcendental conditions, but a grammatological one, where reason is an open-ended and quasi-transcendental affirmation of the coming of what we cannot see coming, of the unenclosability of singular things within fixed bounds. On Kant's idea of reason, reason imposes conditions; on Derrida's idea of reason, reason exposes everything conditioned, including reason itself, to the unconditional. In this case, Derrida suggests, the distinction between faith and knowledge, and therefore between religion and secularity, is far more porous than people like Kant were prepared to believe back in the Enlightenment, and this is because the unconditional opens up both reason and faith alike to something they cannot see coming. There is both a theology and a philosophy of the unconditional and it is not at all clear what the distinction is between them or whether we should even be bothered to draw one.

Clearly everything depends upon maintaining the tension between the rules and the unruly, striking the right or optional mix between conserving the rules and promoting the event. Too much conservation spells death to the institution or tradition, death by rigidification or calcification. Too much event-ing also spells death—madness, trauma, and chaos, and so brings on a death by dissipation. James Joyce proposed a felicitous formulation of the way around too much order (cosmos) and too little (chaos) with the magnificent locution "chaosmos," which we might describe as an optimal state of disequilibrium, adding just the right dash of madness to get an optimized dis/order, in/stability, an/archy, which is deconstruction in a nutshell.

## The Undeconstructible

It therefore should not be difficult to understand that, contrary to its critics, deconstruction is not simply fooling around, not simply mad, not a simple anarchy, that it takes place under the influence of something that holds it in its grip. The next question we must ask then is, what is that? By what is the entire process of deconstruction ordered or commanded? To what is deconstruction loyal? To what is it prepared to swear an oath? What authority does it recognize? What does it affirm? To what is it responsible? To what call does it respond?

The answer is *the undeconstructible*. To any given deconstruction there is a corresponding undeconstructible. To any given order in which a deconstruction is undertaken—like the deconstruction of religion—there is something undeconstructible in that order (in religion, for example) which serves as that for the sake of which the deconstruction is undertaken, something that inspires it and demands it. There is of course no such thing as Deconstruction, capitalized and in the singular, just so many different deconstructive analyses—of literary works, political systems, institutional organizations, historical traditions, political constitutions, philosophical positions—each of which has something undeconstructible in mind, motivating it, inspiring it. Any given deconstructive analysis then is undertaken with unremitting loyalty to the undeconstructible, which is also the very reason a construction is always deconstructible, since no construction ever gets that far. So to the two theses of deconstruction we stated above we can now add a third:

3. Deconstructibility arises both from below, from the inscription of any construction in space and time, and also, and more interestingly, from above, from the pressure exerted by the undeconstructible under which any and every construction breaks down.

That is why Derrida will say that the undeconstructible is the unconditional—this is not my imagination; this is the very language of *both* Derrida and Tillich—whereas the conditional is what is constructed under the concrete conditions of language, history, and the socio-political order. The conditional exists in space and time; it is actual and factual, real and historical. The unconditional, on the other hand, is what we are dreaming of, what we are praying for, what we desire with a desire beyond desire:

• The unconditional is what makes demands upon *us* (in the accusative), unconditionally. The unconditional is what we are provoked by, what is calling to us and to which we respond.
• The unconditional is what *we* (now in the nominative) affirm unconditionally; what we are loyal to, without being in a position to set forth prior conditions or demands.

The unconditional is more what has us than something we have. When it comes to the unconditional, the unconditional always comes first and we never have the initiative. Even when we affirm the unconditional, in the nominative, that affirmation comes second, in response to the prior call the unconditional has paid us. In that sense, before we are a "we," we are an "us," the ones who are called upon (*tois kletois*, 1 Cor 1:24). The undeconstructible, then, is an unconditional call to which we are called upon to respond, in the accusative, and that is the authority to which we are responsible. Deconstruction is not anarchy but a theory of responsibility; it is not anything goes but a matter of loyalty to the call, which has a tripartite structure corresponding to the tripartite structure of time: the call is what is calling to us now; what is being called for (to come); what we are asked to recall.

The notion of the call is central to deconstruction and I will say more about it below (chapter 8). Suffice it for the moment to say that the call is what is visited upon us without our asking for it; the call is uncalled for. It is not our doing, but what is being done to us. The world has started without us. The call is always already embedded in language, history, and tradition, which are already running by the time we arrive on the scene. The call arises from the dual solicitations of an unforeseeable future and an immemorial past. Under the impact of the call, then, any given construction, as something conditioned, as a relatively stable unity of meaning, is destabilized by what is calling, both by the promise of what is being called for and by the memory of the past. The present, Derrida says, is "spooked" by the ones who are to come, *les arrivants*, and the ghosts of the past, *les revenants*, which is another word for the ghosts of the "returned." Together these ghosts make up a "hauntology,"[20] or let's say a kind of haunto-theology! In deconstruction, we are situated like Hamlet being spooked by the ghost of his father, or like old Scrooge being spooked by the ghosts of Christmas past, present, and future. The spooks are trying to deconstruct Ebenezer's miserable life, which means they are trying to do him a favor, painful as it may seem to the old curmudgeon. Generally, when something is deconstructed, we should greet it as "good news" and be grateful, even if sometimes it leaves us standing on our beds in the middle of the night all atremble.

## The Protestant Principle
## and the Jewish Principle

In order then to join the forces of Derrida's analysis of the unconditional with Tillich's, let us recall what Tillich called the "Protestant Principle," which Tillich greatly expanded beyond denominational Protestantism into a principle by which even historical Protestantism, the "Protestant era," should be judged. He thought this principle was a general principle, generally good advice, for anyone who lives in time (and who does not?), that it could and should accordingly outlive historical Protestantism and last as long as time itself. On Tillich's telling, *semper reformanda* means that nothing finite and conditional can ever be adequate to the infinite and unconditional, which stands in constant judgment over anything finite and conditional—including religion, including even the Protestant one. Derrida proposes his own deconstructive and—let's say—Jewish Principle, let's say *semper deconstruenda*: no construction can ever be adequate to the undeconstructible and so every construction stands under constant judgment by the undeconstructible. Nothing that exists is ever adequate to the pressure of the call of what is being called for. No finite and conditional form must ever be confused with what is being called for. The other side of the Protestant Principle is the *justus et peccator* (justified by faith and sinner), which for Luther was crucial to his theology of the cross, but for Derrida means that we are not big high-powered subjects or autonomous egos that have the power to go around deconstructing things. We do not weaken God or anything else; our only power is to let God be God. We are always being-called upon, in the accusative (*peccator*), and we are asked to embrace the dynamics of a certain faith in what is coming, which is of course being saved (*justus*) by the doubt (incredulity) built into faith.

The near proximity of Tillich's Protestant Principle and Derrida's Deconstructive Principle can be explained by their common biblical credentials in the critique of idolatry. My desire to find a way

beyond theism goes hand in hand with my special interest in focus-
ing upon the idolatry of power, which is where religion and classical
theology need to heed the biblical advice they so freely dispense to
others about false gods. The idol or false God that I take to be of
singular relevance, the one that poses a singular danger to itself and
everyone else, is the God of power, the Supreme Being, the *deus
omnipotens*, half-blasphemous and mythological. The model (and
of course models are always constructed) of "divine sovereignty,"
which has long been the model of, and the best alibi for, political
sovereignty—from God to the Monarch to Men (when I capitalize
things I am mocking them and giving them a hard time)—is what
is most in need of deconstruction.

Divine sovereignty is a construction which reduces the unconditional to a particular historical condition of the world, to one of the
powers and principalities that does combat in the world. It alienates
the freedom of the people of God, reducing them to subjects of an
inscrutable and often short-tempered tyrant, whose fits of temper
go hand in hand with fits of love, which is the paradigm of a really
bad and abusive marriage. It defaces what God's unconditional rule
would look like and falls under the judgment of the unconditional
which commands us not to put constructions before the unconditional. This idolatry reduces us to a situation in which we are not
saved *by* the power of God; we need to be saved *from* the power
of God. So it is in the best interests of theology to feel about for a
way beyond theism and omnipotence, for a certain death of God, a
certain crucified God, that will give the name (of) "God" new life.
That is why I will move from here to defend the weakness of God
(chapters 5–6).

It should by now be clear that the notion that deconstruction is
a purely secular inquiry is suspect in the extreme. In fact, it makes
the very idea of a purely secular critique look suspect, which stands
Marx on his head. Marx said that the critique of the mystifications
of religion is the model for every critique of the mystifications of political ideology. Tillich and Derrida turn the table on Marx and say

that it is not the critique of religion but religion's critique of idols that comes first. The religious critique of everything conditional in the light of the unconditional is the paradigm of every supposedly secular critique, to which Derrida adds that this very prophetic and messianic motif coming straight from the Bible is what lies behind Marx's own critical impulse. As Derrida said, by trying to chase away the fantastic specters of religion, Marx exorcized one ghost too many, namely, the one that he himself invoked, as when he opened *The Communist Manifesto* by saying that the specter of Communism was haunting Europe, which was meant to spook the complacent European bourgeoisie by telling them that Communism was coming to get them![21]

This common prophetic streak shows up in the messianic overtones of Derrida's discussion of democracy, to take but one of many possible examples. Democracy, for Derrida, is always a democracy-to-come. No actual existing democracy is adequate to the pressure that is put on it by what is calling upon us, by what is recalled, and by what is being called for in and under the spooky, spectral, inspiring name of democracy. Democracy is never here, even in the existing democracies. Democracy is always coming, like a Messiah who never shows up but who keeps on disturbing us in the middle of the night with the promise/threat of his coming. Democracy is a memory and a promise, something we are dreaming of, something we are haunted by, something we desire with a desire beyond desire, hoping against hope. Might we even say something we are praying for? I will say more of prayer below (chapter 3).

So conceived, deconstruction does not propose an ontology of what exists, a metaphysics of what is present, but a certain "hauntology" of what is spooking us, of voices coming back from the dead, or luring us from the future, calling from who knows where, calling upon and disturbing us in the night. When we wake, bolt upright in our bed, looking all around, we are sure there was someone in the room. We are certain we heard someone say something. If Heidegger could have brought himself to tell a joke, he might have been led to say that being is spooked by time, that the time is out of joint and the reason is that being is being spooked. That is to say that being or presence is de-stabilized, dis-jointed, made restless by time—while we are the restless ones, the ones whose hearts are restless, *inquietum est cor nostrum*, as Augustine said.[22] It is not only that the times are out of joint, but that time is the out-of-jointness of being.

The way I am wont to put this matter these days is to say that the unconditional does not exist; it insists.[23] The unconditional is a call, and existence is what is called for, while we are called upon to fill up what is missing in the body of the unconditional, which sounds a little bit like St. Paul on the body of Christ (Col 1:24). We are on the receiving end of a call which is visited upon us and puts us in the accusative. As always, we are free either to respond to this call or to try to ignore it, to manage not to notice it, even to positively forget and repress it. We are haunted by this call, spooked and inspired—which means that if we refuse it we fall into despair.

We might even say that the unconditional is in-finite, *not* be-cause it is an infinite being or existent—the unconditional does not exist at all; it insists—but because it is un-finished. Its infinity is in-finitival, always to come, always calling for something to come, like a kingdom, which does not show up. As I will show below, it is not a highest being, or even the ground of beings, or the hyper-being of apophatic theology. Grammatologically, the unconditional is always cast as a grammatical infinitive. Any unconditional *x* is the *x* to come. What has come is actual, existent, present, finite, a con-struction, a relatively stable effect—which is always already exposed to the solicitation of the to-come, where a solicitation means not only an entreaty but, in the literal sense of *sollicitare*, a shaking or agitating, not an immovable imperial power.

# 3

# Proto-Religion

Of what use is it, then, to join the forces of Tillich and deconstruction as a way of getting at the unconditional in religion, God, and theology? To answer that question I propose we think in terms of what I will call here a certain "proto-religion."

Let me begin by recapitulating what I have been saying thus far in the following way. In a haunto-theology, we live lives of *hope*—in the hint of the promise of what is to come, of what is being called for—including the promise of the past, the promise of what has been handed down to us by the past. We live lives of *faith*—in the unforeseeable, in the coming of what we cannot see coming. And, not least, we live lives of *love*—of the unconditional, of the undeconstructible, which we desire with a desire beyond desire, with a very agapaic eros or erotic agape. These three remain, faith, hope and love (1 Cor 13:13).

As you can see, I have just described deconstruction by unapologetically replaying the three well known "theological virtues." To the great scandal of many deconstructors and philosophers—the pious want miracles and the philosophers want arguments (1 Cor 1:22)—I foolishly embrace language that is transparently religious, even theological. I make no excuses. Here I stand. I cannot do otherwise. As a philosopher, I confess that I have been beguiled by theology, tricked into eating of the forbidden fruit by a serpentine seducer, even though I set out on my philosophical career with a clear mind and sober purpose. It is a moment of madness, a matter of weakness: I have never been able *not* to speak of religion, God, and theology, try as I might. I have been hearing these voices all my life. Thus have I been led by the deconstruction of religion to adopt

a language that is patently religious. But be warned in advance, this
may not be the religion you expect.

## The Pure Folly
## of a Proto-Religion

The theologians distinguish the three theological virtues from the
four cardinal virtues (prudence, justice, fortitude, and temper-
ance). The cardinal virtues, derived from the Latin *cardo*, meaning
hinge, are ways of negotiating with everything conditioned and
constructed, four ways of feeling about for the possibilities that are
embedded in the clusters of actualities in mundane experience, for
the openings that are available in the prose of the world.[24] They
look for the mean between too much and too little, seeking what
is possible in the actual, trying to see what the situation demands.
But if the cardinal virtues are the virtues of the hinged, these other
virtues must be the virtues of the unhinged. If the cardinal virtues
seek the possible, the theological virtues—shall we say, the radical
theological virtues—are tuned to the impossible. If the cardinal
virtues seek the mean state between too much and too little, the
theological virtues go to excess. If the cardinal virtues are the virtues
of a sane and measured life, the theological virtues are slightly mad,
pure folly, practicing the virtues of the spooked—of those who are
haunted by the unforeseeable, the undeconstructible, the unconditional, the impossible.

The theological virtues are the virtues of people who are held
captive by the spell of the unconditional, by the magic of the impossible. While Aristotle's practical wisdom (*phronesis*) refers to the
skill of negotiating with great delicacy among the conditioned circumstances in which we live, the theological virtues always add the
elixir, the magic touch, the leaven of the unconditional, of taking a
risk where not everything is measured, where there is always a touch
of excess, an added bit of madness and folly. When Mary explains to
the angel Gabriel that this is madness, that she could not possibly

be with child, the angel (whose supreme angelic intelligence seems
to include foreknowledge of the coming of Tillich and Derrida) tells
her that with the unconditional, all things are possible, even the
impossible. The name of God has from time immemorial been the
name of the possibility of the impossible.

Let us call these virtues the folly of a "proto-religion," one that
takes place prior to the division into "religious" and "secular" in
the more familiar sense, belonging to a religious *prius* that lies at
the very core—or down in the depths—of our experience. Here
we are cashing in our desire to dig deeper rather than to try to fly
higher, to feel about for what is underlying, for a religion that is
more deeply lodged. This is a religion that Tillich calls a matter of
"ultimate concern," of our deepest concerns, where he says we are
seized by being-itself, and that Derrida called a "religion without
religion," meaning a kind of religion without the long robes. This
is a religion without a Supreme Being and angelic astronauts deliv-
ering messages from the God to maidens down here on earth, that
does without the accouterments of the confessional or historical
religions, like the Lutheran church in which Tillich was raised or
the synagogue Derrida's mother made him attend as a child. That
does not mean this proto-religion is an ahistorical cross-cultural
universal. God forbid! I am not saying that if we dig deep enough
into the different we will find that everything is the same. Far from
it. If we put different kinds of dough in the same oven, the same
heat will produce different kinds of bread. So in saying that these
are deep or basic, I am saying they are deep or basic hermeneutic
and phenomenological structures, that is, basic to our particular
historical experience, and in saying that they are structures, I am
saying that these are structures of excess and hence that they de-
structure, that they open things up and keep the future open. They
have been constructed in and by the special historical existence of
those who recognize themselves in it. This means that in their core
every *homo* with a history like "ours" (there's the rub), is a *homo*

*religiosus.* If "we" (who?) had a different history, we might not talk like this at all—about God, religion or theology; about the messianic, democracy, etc. Lots of people do not. In deconstruction, keep your guard up, or even head for the door, every time someone says "we" or "our."

The prose of the world, the make-up of our familiar, quotidian existence, is a cluster of conditioned and constituted things which together make up the field of what is actual. But this field of actualities is framed about by horizons of expectation, so that it is surrounded by a ring of possibility. When we turn the corner we expect to find the stately old bank that has stood there for years, not a sea of burning sulfur. When we sink from exhaustion into our favorite chair, we expect it to hold us up. Our horizons of expectation form the border of the future that we can more or less foresee, upon which we rely, and for which we can prepare. We save for our old age or for the children's education, and it would be irresponsible not to do so. Let us call that the "future present," meaning the future we foresee becoming present.

But then there is always the future we cannot see coming—we might not make it to old age, our favorite old chair finally collapses, they tore down the old bank while we were out of town—the future for which we cannot prepare, which we can call the "absolute future." Sometimes things happen that shatter our horizon of expectation—in ways both little and large, for better or for worse. The future brings us gifts, but some gifts are poison. Some unforeseen changes represent terrible setbacks in the search for justice, just as there are astonishing advances. There are profound shifts in art and in science, groundbreaking transformations that leave everyone reeling—asking is this even art? Or science? How is such a thing possible? These are moments of madness, sheer folly.[25] That is what Derrida calls *the* impossible, not logically impossible, like (*p* & not-*p*), but phenomenologically, like something we just cannot believe. When something like this happens in science or in art, we just shake our heads and say, this is madness. The unconditional, then, is not only in-finite or infinitival, but impossible, shattering the ring of possibility, leaving us unhinged. This is the subject or reference point of another kind of responsibility, where we are asked to respond to the call of the coming of a future that we cannot see coming, to prepare to be surprised, to prepare to be unprepared. Here we are summoned to be loyal to the unconditional, enjoined to respond without evasion to the undeconstructible, to affirm the possibility of the impossible, to let the prose of the present world be disrupted by the poetry of a world to come.

Clearly, theology and religion in the familiar sense or, as Derrida puts it, what "we" call religion "in Christian Latin" (or theology in Christian Greek), are concrete historical effects. Religion does not drop from the sky. It belongs to the sphere of constituted, conditioned actualities, not of the unconditional. Religion is produced by the various cultural matrices, social, political, linguistic. That is why the work that has been done in recent years on the history of the word religion is so important. Religion, both the word and the history, can be made into a scholarly object, etherized and stretched out on a table, as T. S. Eliot put it. Religion is a construction, somewhat in the sense that Karl Barth says that religion is what we do while revelation is what God does (although I do not think that the latter part of that distinction holds up in quite those terms, but that is another matter).[26] By describing deconstruction in terms of a more deep-set or elemental faith, hope, and love, of the virtues of the unhinged, I have been speaking of deconstruction in terms that are clearly saturated with the discourse of religion. I am even claiming that deconstruction is structured like a religion—albeit a proto-religion of the undeconstructible and of the possibility of the impossible, which is why it can lend a considerable hand to a theology of the unconditional. These structures of the impossible permeate—or so they should—everything we do, all of our beliefs and practices, institutions and traditions. There is an underlying passion for the impossible, a deeper affirmation of the unconditional not only in religion, but also in the arts and the sciences, in ethics and in politics—lacking which these forms of life are lifeless and inert, would make no progress, and would sag into an endless repetition of the same.

This logic—or better para-logic—of the impossible underlies, or so it should, *all* of our beliefs and practices, including religion. This para-logic, which seems to trade in folly, is the subject matter of a more radical theology that lies at the core of the various confessional theologies, which in the main take the form of a "high" or "strong" theology of the Supreme Being. This brings us to what I think is Tillich's most radical claim, indeed the founding claim of a "radical theology," which goes under the name of what he called a "theology of culture." If we ask Tillich where are theology and religion found, where is their subject matter, in what are they interested, the answer is *not* up above, in the heavens, but down here in the culture. But a theology of culture does not mean applying theology as a prior and independent enterprise *to* culture, but that theology *is* a theology of culture, an analysis of the depth dimension *in* culture, of what is deepest about our culture, our cultural lives, our beliefs and practices, ourselves. The culture then is not secular but always already theological. Alternately, since the literal sense of secular is "the age" (from the Latin *saeculum* ), we could perfectly well speak of a "secular theology," which would mean the theology lodged in the depth of the cultural life of the age, those points in the culture where the culture is glowing white hot, where the unconditional has been engaged in radical works of art, literature, science, politics, etc.

## Two Examples

Where can such a proto-religion be found? Anywhere. Anytime we are left shaking our heads, saying to ourselves, this is madness. In fact, the very existence of religion as a *separate* sphere of cultural life, as contained within a separate space—say as the private from the public, or the religious from the secular—is testimony to our alienation, to the uprootedness of our lives and our severing from what is going on in the depths or at the core of our experience. I hasten to point out in passing that this partitioning or boxing off of life is a paradigmatic gesture of "modernity," and that breaking open these boxes is the best excuse I can think of for retaining the word "post-modern," even though I admit that this word has been beaten senseless by overuse. The para-logic of the unconditional, where the impossibility of an experience is transformed into an experience of the impossible, goes to the heart of cultural life in all its varieties. If religion has a specific identity, if it can be marked off and confined within identifiable cultural boundaries, then we are alienated from the religion that is going on in what Tillich calls the ground of our being or what Derrida calls the domain of the event. So this proto-religion is found everywhere—inside religion and outside, with religion and without, which is the formulation favored by Derrida who explores the strange logic of the "without," of the *sans*, which erases something or crosses it out while leaving traces of it still legible under the erasure (*sous rature*). Proto-religion could then, in principle, live on, survive, without the "confessional" re-ligious traditions by which we are currently surrounded. Life does not lose its depth if people walk away from religion; in fact, many times, it is necessary to protecting life against religion.

To make this point clear, to show what such a proto-religion of the unconditional would actually look like and that it could be found anywhere, let me give you two examples, two places in the culture where we find religion lurking where we did not expect to find religion at all.

The first we can call the "courage to be," borrowing from the title of one of Tillich's most famous books. The example comes from the story, evidently true, of the string quartet that continued to play its music as the Titanic sunk into the cold waters of the North Atlantic in the early morning hours of April 15, 1912. That was certainly an exercise of remarkable courage in a recognizably moral or ethical sense. So it looks like I might have chosen one of

the classical cardinal virtues when I was trying to illustrate a quasi-
or proto-theological virtue. It is completely true that this was a
remarkable show of moral courage, unselfish and unafraid. Who
among us would have been able to act like that if put in the same
circumstances? It took tremendous courage, profound courage. But
it is the "profound" that interests me here, the depth dimension,
the excess, for there is something more going on here, something
uncontainable contained in what they did. Why would these four
people do that? Why were they not running around like everyone
else trying to save their hides, to get on a life-boat, maybe even
elbowing out the competition as there were not enough life boats
to go around? How very foolish! Were they mad? What were they
thinking of? They did not expect to win a raise in salary from their
employer for their fidelity to their job. They were not trying to
become famous, as they could have had no idea that anyone would
ever learn of their story. As fate would have it, they did in fact
acquire a certain immortality—we remember what they did with
awe—but that I wager was the last thing on their mind.

Here they were, faced with catastrophe, continuing to play their
beautiful music. Here they were, faced with certain and horrendous
death, affirming the unconditional beauty of their music, affirming
its power—a power without the power to lift them off that boat.
Here they were, affirming the unconditional value of life in the face
of death. If they wanted to be morally altruistic, would it not have
made more sense to have abandoned their instruments and helped
the women and children on to the life-boats? That would have been
the *practical* thing to do, the sensible thing, to do what is *possible*,
which is the mark of the well-hinged cardinal virtues. Instead, they
chose to stand at their posts, as loyal and courageous as any soldier
in the face of danger, in order to do the impossible. This was mad
and plainly foolish and it wasn't going to save anyone. Their music
wasn't going to keep the ship afloat. Any fool could have told
them that. But they were saying to everyone who could hear, this
is what life will have been; this foolishness is why we live in the first

place. This is what Tillich calls the courage to be, where over and above (or buried deep within) the exercise of an ethical or moral courage, there is also a kind of ontological courage, which affirms being unconditionally, foolish though it may be from the point of view of the good sense of the world, allowing itself to be seized by the powerless power of being itself. That is what Tillich means by religion and what I mean by a proto-religion of the unconditional and by the folly of God. But it has nothing to do with religion in the narrow or strict sense, nothing to do with supernatural beings, churches, divine revelations, resurrected bodies, dogmas and long robes. It may well be—in fact it would be perfect for my purposes— that all four men were atheists. That would in fact intensify their religion.

My second example is Derrida, who wrote a little half-book entitled "Circumfession," a quasi-Augustinian, slightly atheistic, rather Jewish counterpart to Augustine's *Confessions*, which con- stitutes something of a postmodern proto-confessions, one crucial result of which—in the best tradition of Tillich—is to displace the distinction between theism and atheism.[27] It is important to see that Derrida, who "quite rightly passes for an atheist" and a secular philosopher—up to the 1990s, at least—does not use the occasion to launch an Enlightenment assault or attack upon religion. Nor did he, in the manner of Heidegger, show how philosophy can "correct" theology.[28] Deconstruction is not a superior "correction" of theology; nor is it a drive-by shooting in the manner of the new atheists. While religion deserves criticism—what does not?—and deconstruction has several critical things to say about religion—who does not?—deconstruction is not a Critique of Religion, in the manner of Kant, Marx or Freud or the (not so very) new atheists. What Derrida does do is situate, even insinuate, himself inside the *Confessions*, adopt its standpoint, attempt to occupy the position of Augustine and *repeat* the *Confessions*, reinvent the event that takes place in the *Confessions*, restaging it or replaying it. That, if I may say so, is a vintage "postmodern" gesture.

When Derrida jokes that he and Augustine are "compatriots" he first of all is referring to an accident of birth. He was born in Algeria (ancient Numidia), in the suburbs of Algiers, about three hundred miles from ancient Hippo (modern Annaba), where Augustine served as Bishop until his death in 430, which took place exactly 1500 years before Derrida's birth. But he also means that he and Augustine are compatriots of the unconditional, both praying and weeping over the event, the possibility of the impossible—Augustine in the premodern setting of ancient (North African) Christianity, Derrida in the postmodern setting of a leftist, secular, Jewish, Left Bank Parisian intellectual who inherited a Greco-European tradition of philosophy. In "Circumfession" the distinctions between theism and atheism, theology and philosophy, faith and reason, the religious and the secular, weaken, wither, and finally fall away. Theism and atheism belong to the level of opposing confessional, conditional, constituted "beliefs"; they fail to get as far as the more elemental and affective "faith" in the unconditional, in the coming of what we cannot see coming that we have been describing. They fail to get as far as the folly of this proto-religion.

The reason this restaging of the *Confessions* is so very surprising—with all the shock of the unforeseeable event—is that the *Confessions* is a prayer. While widely considered the first autobiography, which is not entirely untrue, the book is actually, upon a closer consideration of its literary genre, a prayer. If we were to stage the original scene of the *Confessions*, Augustine's back would be turned to us because he is addressing God, turned to "you" (*tu*), a word which, as Peter Brown points out, is to be found in 381 of its 453 paragraphs,[29] which means that we readers are overhearing a man at prayer. The utterly surprising thing about Derrida's "Circumfession," therefore, is that in assuming the position of Augustine Derrida also falls to his knees, repeats its prayer and its faith, its confession and its God. Instead of a Critique of Religion, Derrida reinvents and repeats Augustine's religion, restaging in terms of the para-logic of the impossible what is going on in Augustine's *Confessions* but *without* the prayer and the God of confessional Christianity or of the Judaism of his childhood home.

How can that be? Ask yourself, what is *prayer* if not what Jean-Louis Chrétien calls a "wounded word" (*parole blessée*), sighs sent up by a heart wounded and made restless by the unconditional, sighing and weeping over the coming of the unconditional?[30] What is *faith* if not our faith in the hints of a promise, in the coming of the unforeseeable, as opposed to the various "beliefs" maintained in the creedal communities? What is *confession* if not a confession that we are all a little lost, and maybe even a lot, severed or cut (as in circumcision) from absolute knowledge and absolute truth, so that we do not know in any deep way who we are? When we get down to the depths, we are lost in non-knowledge, left to feel around in the dark like a blind man with a stick.

Most centrally—this is our central and underlying interest, theology's interest, and in theology's best interests—what about God? Again, ask yourself, what is *God* if not the possibility of the impossible, the name of the event of the un/conditional, un/deconstructible, *the* im/possible? What is God if not the folly of the impossible? And what better way to describe the condition of this wounded heart than to say with Augustine "our hearts are restless" (*inquietum est cor nostrum*)? What more elemental question can we ask than to ask with Augustine, "what do I love when I love my God?" (*quid ergo amo cum deum meum amo*).[31] Derrida is destabilizing the relatively stable nominal unities that are to be found in the *Confessions*, indeed in conventional religious traditions generally, by exposing the underlying events that take place there. What is going on in and under these conventional religious names in the *Confessions* is being reenacted or reinvented in "Circumfession," replayed or restaged so as to produce new effects, new religious effects in what I am calling, variously, a proto-religion of the unconditional, an affirmative faith in the undeconstructible or impossible, a radical theology or theopoetics of the event that takes place in and under the name (of) "God."

The relation of God to the unconditional, the undeconstructible, the impossible, should by now be clear: the name (of) "God" is one of the ways we give words to the unconditional, one of the ways that the unconditional happens in our lives. The name (of) "God" is a conditioned effect in various natural languages which contains something unconditional, which of course it cannot contain (limit). But it is not the only way. Indeed, for many people—of a different mindset, culture, education, personal history, born in a very different time and place, speaking a different language—it is not available at all. It may very well be unheard of, or an obsolete dead letter, or irredeemably superstitious and supernaturalistic. From the point of view of an analysis of the unconditional, this is no cause for alarm. It simply reflects the various conditions under which the unconditional happens in our lives.

# 4

# How Long
# Will Religion Last?

How long can religion, God and theology be expected to last? Is God dead? Or maybe just a short-timer destined for demise in the near future? I raise this question as a way to bring this discussion to a head. I have been highlighting the depth dimension in religion and throwing doubt on God in the highest by way of the distinction between the conditional and the unconditional, between confessional religious traditions and what I am calling a kind of proto-religion of the unconditional. So, as another way to see the point I am making, let's ask, can religion and theology live on in postmodern times and in whatever "post-" postdates postmodernism? How we answer this depends upon the distinctions we have just made.

## The Priests Always Have Good News

Truth to tell, the confessional traditions and their Supreme Being have exhibited remarkable survival skills. Every time the death of God is announced, a funny thing happens on the way to the funeral. Every time religion is pronounced dead at the scene, religion revives and lives on to bury its own undertakers. Even if you think the resurrection of the dead is a lot of hocus pocus, you have to concede that, however dead they are said to be, religion, God, and theology always manage to return from the dead. The French psychoanalyst Jacques Lacan (1901–81) thinks he knows why. The priests, he says, have an explanation for everything. No matter how grim the forecast; no matter how bloody, terrible, and unjust the past; no matter how murderous the world may become, the priests have an answer.

They can invariably come up with a Big Explanation, a Providential Theory of Everything, God's Long-Term Divine Plan that covers everything, while also insisting, of course, that we ourselves here down below can only see the ways of the God in the sky through a glass darkly. That is what they are trained to do and they are fabulous at it.[32]

The priests always have good news, while psychoanalysis, on the other hand, is left holding the bag, left to break the bad news to us that there is no such big Other (aka, God). Lacan tells us that beneath the reality we have *constructed* in images (the imaginary) and in logic and language (the symbolic)—notice that what Lacan calls "reality" pretty much overlaps with what deconstruction calls a construction and Tillich calls the conditional—which makes the world make sense, there is the uninhabitable world of the unbearably real, where there is no big Other. In a contest with religion, Lacan says, in an exercise of his usual sarcasm, psychoanalysis will always *lose* while the comforting story told by the priests will always win. Religion, the God of religion, Lacan thinks, will last as long as we greet the future with fear and anxiety, which for him means forever. I think his prediction is cynical but nevertheless not a bad one. As there will always be pandering politicians and shady sellers of used cars, so there will always be the comfort-giving God, religious con men and flimflammers, a ready-with-an-answer religion, the God of those for whom the unconditional is reduced to a Supreme Being, a half-blasphemous and mythological Big Being in the sky. The Enlightenment dared us to think, but there will always be a religion and a God for those who wouldn't dare.

But are there any good reasons for religion, or for God, or, to be a bit more exact, for *what is going in the name (of) "God,"* to live on? Might there be a religion that deserves to last and has nothing to do with *winning*? Might there be a religion without that religion and that religion's God, the one Lacan is lambasting? Might there not be a proto-religion that we hope and pray will or should live on, even at the risk of losing? Might there be a religion, which "makes itself worthy of the event that has happened to it?"[33] What event? The promise, the unconditional call of the future. In the place of the crypto-Calvinism of Lacan lamenting our total depravity and of Slavoj Žižek (1949–)[34] lamenting the unredeemable lack in our being, might there be a psychoanalysis of hope in the event? According to the proto-Protestant and slightly Jewish principle of deconstruction, the unconditional (which is embedded in the conditional), the infinite (which is embedded in the finite), can never be exhausted in any conditional finite response to what is being called for unconditionally. That means what is contained *in* religion can never be contained *by* religion, by the varieties of what we call, in Christian Latin English, religion. The various historical confessional religions are just so many conditioned, conditional responses, so many constructions, so many versions of what Hegel called a *Vorstellung*, a kind of palpable depiction or picture, of something unconditional, all arising in response to the call of the unconditional. So whether or not the confessional religions will in fact survive, the unconditional is the element within them which makes them *worthy* of surviving. They can make themselves worthy of this event, and worthy of survival, only if they do not prevent the event; only if they allow themselves to be inwardly disturbed, or haunted from within, by the proto-religious affirmation of the unconditional, by the para-logic of the impossible, to which they give flesh and bones.

More generally, God, the name of God, is but one of our names for the unconditional, for the event of the impossible, because what is contained in the name of the unconditional cannot be contained by the name of God. The subject matter of theology, what is of interest to theology, what is in the best interests of theology, is not God, but the unconditional, one of whose names is God, which is a symbol or a figure of the unconditional. The unconditional can take place under other names. The name of God is one of its names but not the only one.

That does not mean the confessional theologies are to be taken lightly or simply brushed aside. There would not be much of consequence in the unconditional if it did not take place, again and again, under particular and determinate conditions. After all, as a religion without religion this proto-religion of the unconditional has to make do without a central headquarters in the Vatican or Nashville, without a board of elders, churches, prayer books and candles and, perhaps most important of all, without weekly donations! As it lacks the wherewithal to lay down its head, the confessional bodies supply the insistence of the unconditional call with existence, or so they should. In return for this favor, the proto-religion haunts and disturbs the confessional bodies, waking them with a start in the middle of night (like old Scrooge), reminding them that they do not know to whom they are praying or even that there is anyone there to whom to pray; reminding them that their confessional response to the call is but one of many possible responses to a call of ambiguous provenance. This interplay, this porous interpenetration of the one by the other—of confessional theology and radical theology, of religion and a proto-religion, of the conditional and the unconditional—results in a destabilization, a deconstruction of the confessional theologies by the insistent voice of a spooky spectral figure, by an uncanny unconditional call, a call calling for the madness and foolishness of the event. Or so it should; that is their best excuse for surviving. The future of the confessional traditions is bound up with a willingness to expose themselves to the absolute future, to the unforeseeable, to allow themselves to be haunted by the insistence of the unconditional call. Lacking this exposure they will be nowhere to be found among the dare-to-think set and will flourish only under the lamentable conditions Lacan sarcastically describes. They will survive, live on, but without life, as so many ways to prevent the event.

## Is Religion Worthy of Lasting?

So the question, Will religion last? should be reformulated, Is religion *worthy* of lasting? I would venture to say that the proto-religion of the unconditional that I have been describing is a religion worthy of having a future just because the future is its very subject matter. It has to do with the very momentum of our being, our being catapulted—let us say our catapulsion—into the unconditional call of the future. It has to do with the very futurity or futural being of human experience, with the very structure of our experience as beings of and in time. The pulse of this pulsation can be found in religion in the narrow sense; when it is not, it should be. But even when it is, it cannot be confined there. It is found everywhere in the culture; when it is not, it should be, in accord with Tillich's theology of culture. The para-logic of the impossible, the affirmation of the unconditional, which lies at the core of our experience, seems to me irreducible. A good many conservative confessional traditions, maybe most, do their best to limit this exposure, to prevent the event, with the intent of protecting orthodoxy, but many radical open-ended welcoming communities do their best to maintain this exposure, with the intent of protecting the unconditional. Either way, with or without what has been called religion in the usual sense, I can see a theology *in* the future which would be a theology *of* the future, a theology of hope,[35] a theology-to-come and a generation of coming theologians, who would make up a proto-religion of the unconditional promise, which is a way to say, even to pray, "come" to the coming of what we cannot see coming, which is risky business.

The death of the God of high and mighty theology is good news. But if the name of God is the name of the unconditional, then the death of *that* God is bad news. The death of the God without God will take place only at the expense of the futurity of experience itself, at the expense of preventing the event. I am not saying that this could not happen. It certainly could. It would take place with the victory of the programmable, the foreseeable, which is the old debate in which the post-structuralists were first engaged. This debate has resurfaced today in an ominous form under the name of what is often called "post-humanism," which has itself an oddly theological longing for immortality, for becoming a little less than the angels to the point of making up the difference altogether. Will the post-human open up a new post-human future or will it mean that everything will be programmed, written, and prescribed in advance, in our genetic codes and computer codes and who know what else? Will Derrida's open-ended grammatology succumb to a universal programmatology? If so, then what is hopeful in every promise, and risky in every threat, would be programmed away. Every faith and hope and love would be written out of the human script. That would be the end of religion in the most radical sense I can imagine. And where is it written that that cannot happen?

As there is much at stake, we are reduced to a prayer, left to hang on by a prayer. Let us pray like mad for religion and theology and for God! Let us pray for a theology-to-come, for a kingdom-to-come, as a realm of endless open-endedness, of endless exposure, to the possibility of the impossible. If we were ancient Greeks, we would build a temple to the unconditional on this very spot. Absent that, let us offer a prayer to and for the coming of this kingdom, a prayer that restages the penultimate line of the New Testament, replaying the prayer "Come, Lord Jesus" offered at the end of the book of Revelation. Let us offer an even more lost and wounded word, offering a prayer for the coming of the event, a *viens, oui, oui,* come, yes, yes, come, yes, I said yes, come, amen, alleluia, yes. Then let us keep our fingers crossed, for it takes a certain madness, a divine folly, to call for the coming of what we cannot see coming.

# 5

# In Praise of Weakness

Thus far I have been arguing that, as the interest of theology lies not in God in the highest but in the unconditional, the best interests of theology are served if it is not so high and mighty, if it cuts a wide swath around what Tillich calls the half-blasphemous and mytho-logical concept of a celestial being and seeks instead to find the kingdom of God within us, "down" in the depths of our being and of God's. I want now to turn to weakness, to say a word on behalf of weakness—meaning both the weakness of God and of the weak theology that gives words to God, to what is going on in the name (of) "God." Only then will I be satisfied that the high and mighty God and its companion theology have been cut down to size.

In the interests of transparency, allow me to say up front I am not opposed to any and every exercise of strength. I am not advocat-ing being weak in every sense of the word, like leading an anemic, weak-kneed indecisive life. What I mean by weakness requires a considerable courage, which we have just seen in our discussion of what Tillich called the "courage to be." My use of the word has several sources, where the word is being used with no little art and to purposes which I think are propitious for theology. The whole thing, we recall, is a certain felicitous folly, an exercise in fidelity to the folly of God, in which we are feeling around for a deeper way to be wise.

## Weak Thought

I mention first the "weak thought" (*pensiero debole*) of the contem-porary Italian philosopher Gianni Vattimo (1936–), which is his way of criticizing what I am calling the high and mighty tendencies of classical theology and philosophy.[36] So, where classical metaphysics makes a show of setting forth the fundamental structures of reality, the very nature of objective being, the advocates of weak thought more cautiously claim only to have interpretations. When classical epistemology sets forth the "method" for attaining certitude and silencing one's opponents, we on the weak side take sides with open-ended "conversations" that make some headway in a matter that both sides see is complicated. Where classical ethics tends to be of an either/or, black or white, absolute or relativistic, my-way-or-the-highway frame of mind, we weak thinkers think we can get farther with Aristotle's idea of a flexible insight into the idiosyncrasies of the singular situation and saving inflexible unyielding universals for mathematics. When classical political theory announces authoritarian totalitarian principles, like the classless society or the glory of the *Volk*, we are of a mind to let messier and more democratic processes work themselves out in local, national, and international assemblies.

In each case, "strong" principles are exclusionary and are being allowed to wither into weaker and more open-ended ones. This accords nicely with our Protestant-Jewish principle that nothing conditional, meaning nothing actual and factual, should ever succumb to the illusion that it is strong enough to stand up and be the match for the unconditional. Weak thought for Vattimo is summed up in the word hermeneutics, the theory of interpretation, in the tradition of Heidegger and Hans-Georg Gadamer (1900–2002), while for Richard Rorty (1931–2007), Vattimo's sometime American partner in conversation, it is called "non-foundationalism." Whatever it is called, weak thought is an attempt to find a felicitous way to negotiate between the extremes that are at war in the hardball polarization of absolutism-versus-relativism. In general, when the high and mighty loudly proclaim their absolutes, we weak thinkers head for the exits, preferring instead to speak more softly of interpretations, on the simple grounds that absolutes are always somebody's version of the absolute, somewhere, sometime. These so called absolutes always have an identifiable pedigree, that is, they are always very conditioned constructions trying to pass themselves off as having dropped from the sky, just the way upon closer examination universals invariably turn out to be a local favorite. The panicked right wing thinks that weak thought leads to relativism and anything goes violence, which would be an amusing objection were violence not so serious a matter. After all, the problem with Hitler and Stalin was not that they were relativists. The facts on the ground are that the worst violence ensues, not from hermeneutics, but from resisting hermeneutics, as when someone confuses (their) conditionals with the unconditional, which pretty much comes down to someone who confuses himself with God, which weak thought hopes to discourage on the grounds that it is a very dangerous illusion.

As a young man, Vattimo was a devout daily-Mass-and-the-sacraments Catholic—a devout but gay, fervent but progressive and left of center Catholic, and this understandably caused him no little trouble with the Roman Church. In his later writings, we can see a kind of return to his Catholicism, but a return that took a more postmodern turn and of a much more radical sort. He undertakes in these works a "weakening" of God, which takes its point of departure from Paul's notion of *kenosis*, in which the high and mighty God of strong theology is emptied out into the world without remainder. That the transcendent omnipotent God is "weakened" into the world clearly goes back to Hegel—and to the medieval Italian mystic and theologian Joachim of Fiore (1135–1202), of whom Vattimo is fond—whose philosophical theology also lay at the basis of the "death of God" theologies of the 1960s, of which Vattimo's later thought is strongly reminiscent. The death of the high and mighty God is the birth of God in the world, whose democratic sense of freedom and equality incarnate the divine life today. Where is God? God has pitched his tent in the world, in the depths of the world, in the arts and sciences, in ethical and political life, where the world is busy making the kingdom of God come true, making the name (of) "God" come true in the sacrament of the world. The so-called secular world is the realization of the kingdom of God, not its obliteration, which closely resembles what Tillich means by a "theology of culture," or what is sometimes called a "secular theology," meaning a theology of the *saeculum*, of the age.

## A Weak Messianic

The decisive source of my advocacy of the word weak is Derrida, which is in fact where my whole idea of weak theology got started. Derrida analyzes what he calls the "unconditional without sovereignty," something that makes an unconditional claim on us but without the sovereign power to back it up, something binding but with no power to hold us to it. If you insist on using the old etymology of religion as binding-back, then this religion would be a certain kind of binding without the power to bind with the strong force of real worldly power. That is why Derrida also describes the unconditional as a "weak force."[37] The university, for example, is unconditional—it is the unconditional, unlimited, uncompromisable right to ask any question—but the university as such, if there is such a thing, is without sovereignty. It runs up against all the forces of the actual world which prevail against it, the forces of the government, the church, the free market, and benefactors more interested in funding basketball than the library, all of which try to monitor both the questions that it raises and above all the answers that it renders.[38]

In 1989 Derrida gave a famous lecture to the Cardozo Law School in New York City in which he took up a distinction made by Pascal between the "force of law" and the call for justice.[39] It is the law that has all the force—the institutions, the courts, the police, the militias, the jails—while justice is but a "call" whose voice is ever soft and low. Its call is, to be sure, unconditional, unlimited, uncompromisable, but of itself, it lacks the long, strong arm of the law. The law is what exists, what is actual, effective, and real, while justice does not so much exist as insist, which is how I like to put it. Justice is not so much a reality as a call, a peal or appeal, for something just to become real. Justice without the law is impotent; the law without justice is a tyrant. Hence, Pascal concludes, since we cannot make justice (a call) strong (an existing being), we must make what is strong (the law) just. We must seek to make just laws, to make the call of justice come true in the law. But every such existing (positive) law will be a construction, and as such must be repealable and appealable, that is, deconstructible, otherwise it will become a monster. But the peal of "justice in itself, if there is such a thing" (which there is not), is not deconstructible. Justice is always calling, always pealing and appealing, always to-come. Justice is like a coming Messiah who never quite shows up, not so long as we live in time and history, not so long as there is a future, and when is there not? The Messianic call of justice pays a call upon the present, disturbing and interrupting it, haunting and spooking it, soliciting and destabilizing it, with its unfulfilled expectation for justice for the least among us.

But if the present is disturbed and destabilized by the call coming from the future it is no less disrupted by the solicitations of the past, by what demands to be recalled. That brings us to the other side of messianicity, which is found in the work of Walter Benjamin (1892–1940), a brilliant thinker with an interest in Jewish mysticism who contributed to postmodern theory on several different fronts, who speaks of a "weak messianic power."[40] Benjamin is where Derrida himself picked up the trope of weakness. By a weak messianic Benjamin means that instead of waiting for a (strong) Messiah who will bail us out, *we* are the messianic age. *We* are the ones who have all along been expected—by the dead. *We* occupy the messianic position—to make right the wrongs that have been done to them. But our messianic powers are weak. We cannot make the dead live again. We cannot alter the past and restore them to a life in which they will not have suffered these wrongs or will have been compensated for them. So we can at best remember them, recall them, mourn them with an impossible mourning, by righting the unjust conditions now from which they suffered then, by seeing to it that, as Abraham Lincoln said, their death will not have been in vain. The unconditional call of justice resonates not only with the promise of the justice-to-come but also with the promise of the past, which sounds like a very foolish hope. The present is haunted not only by the ones to come (*les arrivants*) and but also by the "returned" (*les revenants*) who have come back to spook us, spectral figures both, both lacking bodily force, to be sure, but not, for all that, any less unnerving, and maybe more.

## The Weakness of God

That brings me to my third source, the one we started with, the most authoritative from the point of view of the high and mighty theology with which I am contending—St. Paul. In 1 Corinthians 1:18–31 Paul, the apostle lays out the logic of the weakness of God, in preference to the power of the world, and the logic of the folly of God, in preference to what the world calls wisdom, which I think are the touchstones of a theology that Jesus would recognize:

> But God has chosen people the world regards as fools to expose the pretension of those who think they know it all, and God has chosen people the world regards as weak to expose the pretensions of those who are in power. (1 Cor 1:27)

Paul tells us he never laid eyes on Jesus in the flesh but that does not prevent him from capturing in stunning fashion exactly what Jesus was preaching under the name of the "kingdom of God," which Paul calls the logic of the cross. The logic or the rule when God rules is the cross. We will need to keep this uppermost in our mind when we return to the question of what the God in the kingdom of God means at the conclusion of these reflections (chapters 9–10). This use of "logos," as we have said, would have stuck in the craw of the philosophers (the elite) at Corinth for whom the cross is both the substance and the symbol of folly, weakness, death, defeat, and abject humiliation. But Paul argues that God uses the folly of the cross to shame the wisdom of the philosophers, that God makes use of the nothings and nobodies (*ta me onta*) of the world to confound the powers that be. Paul must have known that his use of the vocabulary of "being" (*to on*), logos and wisdom would have maddened the philosophers. He says that the folly of God is wiser than human wisdom and that "the weakness of God" is stronger than human strength. God, the name (of) "God," what is going on in and under the name of God, is God's solidarity with the nobodies not with the Big Deals, with the nothings not the people of substance, with the ill born not the well born, with weakness not with strength, with folly not wisdom.

Now, much as I love this text, far be it from me to try to strong-arm the strong theologians with the authority of the Apostle. In radical theology, the authority of St. Paul is an authority without force, without the force of law, without the *real* terrestrial force that is powered by an ideology of biblical inerrancy or papal infallibility to back it up. There are several versions of "Paul" and there are no terrestrial police to enforce any particular version of what Paul is saying.[41] There is likewise, in radical theology, no celestial being whispering in his ear for whom Paul provides a mouthpiece, so that he is likewise deprived of heavenly force. My Paul speaks for himself—and he usually does this very well indeed—albeit always in response to what is calling upon him. Depriving Paul of both terrestrial and celestial force is the condition under which anything unconditional might be taking place in Paul's appeal to weakness. Otherwise Paul is reduced to the authoritarianism of the long robes.

That is why, in the name of my love of Paul, I am sometimes constrained to disagree with Paul, which for some people means I am destined for ruin but for me simply means that I am not a party to the ruinous mythological and half-blasphemous idols of biblical inerrancy and ecclesiastical infallibility. Paul was, for example, obviously in error about his belief that the coming of the kingdom was imminent. What I am offering under the name of "weak theology" might be seen as systematically thinking through Paul's version of the weakness of God, thinking it radically, all the way down. I think Paul goes very far with his thought of folly and weakness but not far enough, because I think he takes what he says in 1 Corinthians 1 and largely walks it back in 1 Corinthians 2. The ones who are mature and well versed in God's ways (*teleiois*, 1 Cor 2:6) know the secret of which the ones who have earthly power are deprived. The ones who have the *pneuma* know that God's power will out, and that the enemies of God will be both outsmarted and punished. In speaking of weakness and folly, Paul has something up his sleeve. He is entering them into an economy, in which the present weak and low-born status of the Corinthian church will be reversed, and God in all his apocalyptic power will triumph. As New Testament scholar Dale Martin says, "Ultimately, what Paul wants to oppose to human power is not weakness but divine power (2:5)—that is, power belonging to the other realm."[42] The rulers of the world who crucified Jesus will get their come-uppance. They are coming to nothing, and had they known better they would never have crucified him. The wisdom and power of God are going to lay low the so-called wisdom of the powers and the principalities. Paul never shrinks from a fight.

In short, you either get on board with Paul's Christ crucified or you will fry. How does he know that? He has had a Revelation (in the upper case), a very Strong Vision, seen it, been told it in no uncertain terms, in his own personal vision. So the weak theology sketched in the first chapter of 1 Corinthians is an investment that is shown to pay dividends in the second chapter. Weakness is but a preparation for the final staging of an extremely strong theology—when the God of Abraham will be all in all, the Jews first, then the Gentiles ("pagans"). But woe unto those who do not get on board at either stop. Paul does not take the weakness and folly of God as sufficient unto itself, as speaking for itself, as unconditional without power, but as a way to usher in the coming triumph of a very strong God, who is about to establish his kingdom on earth and run circles around worldly wisdom. Paul has apocalyptic power up his apostolic sleeve. When God establishes his rule here on earth, and Paul was mistakenly convinced that this was to be soon in the coming, there will nothing weak or foolish about it.

## Weakness All the Way Down

To think the weakness and folly of God all the way down would consist, accordingly, in resisting the temptation to enter them into an economy of long-term strength and wisdom. It would be to trust weakness without calculating that it will have a long-term pay off in real power (be it earthly or heavenly), when the weak will finally get to pull the trigger and lay low their enemies and God's, which are usually pretty much the same thing. It would begin by disabusing ourselves of the high and mighty God of strong theology who promises to make our enemies our footstool (Ps 110:1), and realizing that the name of God is the name of a weak force, of a call, like justice, which is unconditional but without sovereign power. What would that be like? It would be like forgiveness, which is folly in the light of the world's wisdom, a weak force whose power lies in the power of abdicating power, abdicating retaliation—no footstools—which we might call the power of powerlessness. The power of forgiveness is the utterly disarming power of responding to a wrong done to us not with retribution but with forgiveness. What is that if not madness and folly?

I love Dostoevsky's "Legend of the Grand Inquisitor" for many reasons, but one of the things I love the most about it is the very end. The Lord Cardinal Grand Inquisitor gives a long and quite interesting discourse—which actually make some interesting points that we weak theologians would agree with—in which he makes it absolutely clear that he has all the power in this situation, having the power of life and death over Jesus, and there is no greater power than that. After his eminence concludes his long speech, during which Jesus is completely silent, Jesus does not strike the man dead with a blink of his eye or command his angels to hurl the body of his eminence out of the window crashing it on the plaza below. That is precisely the sort of fantasy with which strong theology nourishes and entertains itself. For the strong theologians, the greatness of Jesus in this scene is his self-restraint, like the strong silent type in the movies whom everyone in the audience knows can level his enemy if he chooses but instead chooses not to. That is why Nietzsche concluded that Christianity was a slave morality spawned by resentment against the powerful. Instead, Jesus simply goes up to the Lord Cardinal and gives him a kiss, which completely disarms the great man, who tells Jesus to leave and never come back. That I think is a splendid distillation of the weakness of God and of how things are done in the kingdom of God, not with a sword but a kiss, and something which the Church, which too often confuses itself with the kingdom of God, as if it were the perfect society, forgets with alarming regularity.

What is so interesting to me is how consistently a so-called secular philosopher like Derrida has explored the paradoxes and madness of a series of "unconditionals" that I think are constitutive of the kingdom of God—like forgiveness and hospitality. Unconditional forgiveness means granting forgiveness *without* laying down the traditional conditions strong theology has always imposed—that the offender express sorrow, make amends, do penance, and promise to offend no more. Such forgiveness would be a little "mad," completely foolish, would it not? As foolish and mad, perhaps, as forgiving one's executioners, as loving one's enemies, as greeting hatred with love. The test case for Derrida was drawn from the depths of his personal experience, namely, the question of the Jews forgiving the Nazis, which was prompted for him by the work of the Jewish philosopher Vladimir Jankélévitch (1903–85), who argued that the Holocaust was "unforgiveable."[43]

The ancient biblical virtue of hospitality represents another and also Jewish example. As a life-long emigrant, who was always being made welcome "elsewhere," as he put it, Derrida had a diasporic, disseminated, and uprooted sense of life. He emphasized the paradox of unconditional hospitality, of welcoming the coming of the stranger "unconditionally," which is of course risky business. Should I answer an insistent and unexpected knock on my door in the middle of the night? Is that not the height of folly? Ought I not to have criteria and conditions set out in advance before doing so? Might this be not a wayfarer in desperate need of help but someone come to harm me? This ambiguity is inscribed in the word *hostis,* the stranger, who might be a "hostile" unless he is a visitor in need of a "host," an ambiguity which Derrida tried to capture by coining the neologism "hosti-pitality."[44] Hospitality is supposed to mean welcoming the other. But normally it means offering hospitality to those whom we have invited, while asking them to be discreet and not mention this invitation to the others, whom we have not invited. So, perversely, hospitality usually turns out to mean welcoming the same and excluding the others. Derrida distinguishes between an invitation, in which we lay down in advance the conditions of a visit, from a visitation, in which someone uninvited shows up, knocking at our door, which is an unconditional call. This unconditional hospitality, like unconditional forgiveness, is much more reminiscent of the unruly rule in the kingdom of God pictured in the parables and sayings of Jesus, which seems like pure folly to the world.

The "kingdom of God," I conclude, turns on the weakness of God. The rule of God is the rule of a weak force, not an *imperium* or *basileia* in the usual sense. The weakness of God is precisely the rule of unconditional calls like forgiveness, hospitality, and the pure gift. God, the *ens supremum,* the celestial being, weakens into the kingdom of God, even as the kingdom of God weakens into the world, into a form of being-in-the-world, a form of life, which is I think what is going on in the incarnationalism of the Incarnation. God, the name of God, the event that takes place in the name (of) "God," represents a way to name what is going on in the kingdom of God, the unruly rule by which the wondrous works of the kingdom are worked. By the impossible everything happens. As I hope it will become clear, not only does the kingdom of God have no need of the *ens supremum*, but were such a God ever to show up, it would ruin everything. That is the issue I will address in the concluding section of this book (chapter 10).

# 6

# Weakening the Being of the Supreme Being

In weak or radical theology, in a theology of the unconditional, the religious conception of God as the Supreme Being, as a powerful agent, a doer of miraculous deeds, is what Hegel called a *Vorstellung*, a picture story, a narrative, a kind of poem, yet not purely a poem—it was more than a work of art—but a deeper story about the meaning of our lives, like a picture postcard of a concept. While the picture postcard serves a purpose for the pious, it is also true that unless and until it becomes cognizant of its pictoriality, classical theology will be—directly in proportion to the extent to which it does not—precisely the mythological and half-blasphemous creature that Tillich is criticizing. So for Hegel the time has come to bring God on high down a peg or two—hence our critique of "on high"—and so allow the might of God Almighty to weaken into something gentler with which we can establish a more amicable relation. Thus would the bombast of a high and mighty God be attenuated into something of a kinder sort, something that would be the genuine interest of theology, an attenuation that attunes it with the best interests of theology.

That poses the task of freeing God from the constellation of power, might and being that has intoxicated theology, what Kierkegaard called "rouged" theology, all powdered and primed and sitting by the window waiting for the powers of the world to

pay it a visit.[45] How else might that task be carried out other than
by letting God weaken into something of a softer, wispier sort,
enacting what for a theologically minded atheism, an atheism with
the best interests of theology in mind, would constitute the "right
religious and theological reply" to the Supreme Being? That is precisely the task I assign a "weak" theology, letting the Being of the
Supreme Being weaken, while keeping in mind when I use the word
weak I am not talking about a pushover. Weakening into what? Into
something that would not be a thing or being but, to borrow the
Jewish philosopher Emmanuel Levinas's cunning phrase, "otherwise than being,"[46] not being but then again not merely nothing.
What Paul called the weakness of God sides with the nothings and
the nobodies, but it is not simply nothing. Far from it. Then what?

That is the task at hand, which I pursue by following up on the
project that Martin Heidegger started under the name of "overcoming metaphysics." That means here filtering out the grains of
metaphysics that have infiltrated theology in order to return to the
lived experience that is obfuscated by the metaphysics. There are
two steps to be taken here, first with respect to Tillich, and the
second with respect to mystical theology, which have to do with the
metaphysical impulses found in both, originating mainly in German
Idealism and Neoplatonism, respectively. Then what will be left
is the unconditional without the power, presence, and prestige of
being, which goes to the heart of what I am calling, or of my gloss
on what Paul is calling, the folly of God.

## Weakening the
## Ground of Being

Tillich's approach thus far has been our guide and point of departure. Tillich seeks to avoid the half-blasphemous and mythological
gesture of orthodoxy, which hypostasizes the ground of being and
personifies the prepersonal ground into a personal doer of mighty
deeds. His atheism may sound like a scandal to the pious and pure
folly to the theologians, a bitter pill to ask theology to swallow

but, like tough love, it is made entirely with God's best interests at heart. Tillich's entire concern is with protecting God's infinity as that in which we finite beings live and move and have our being, a scriptural phrase which I wager he repeated daily. But much as I love Tillich, here I must bid adieu to the God of Tillich and depart from my point of departure. For Tillich, to speak of the ground of being is still to speak of the power of God but in another way, by relocating God's power from a transcendent entity to an underlying force. That is far too strong a thing to say in weak theology, far too loud a boast for our tender ears. Though it may sound like a hard saying, in weak theology it is in God's best interests to deprive God of being the ground of being as well, to swear an oath of fealty to *ta me onta* that goes all the way down—to the ground—and to search for something otherwise than the ground of being or being itself. Tillich and Derrida are agreed that the deconstruction of theology involves showing that the relatively stable (conditioned) unities of meaning that circulate in theology are also relatively unstable (deconstructible). But when Tillich goes on to add that these relatively unstable unities rest upon a deeper stabilizing ground—the ground here meaning a relatively firm support—we cup our ears.

What he means by "depth" is something firmer, and what he means by "ground" is a powerful foundation of a more oblique but nonetheless real sort. In the language of deconstruction, this is to have recourse, albeit on a deeper level, to a philosophy of "presence," that is, of unity, stability, meaning. Presence is *ousia*, being as the underlying reality that outlasts changing appearances. This is not to displace metaphysics, which is the demand for grounds, but simply to defer the arrival of metaphysics, which ultimately shows up at the next stop on the way—in the depth of being, in matters of ultimate concern, in the ultimate ground of being. It does not let the relatively unstable character of things go all the way down to the ground, which would result in more of a groundless ground. That is the disturbance of the notion of ground introduced by deconstruction, which is interested in stressing the contingency of any

construction, including the construction of a ground of the contingent. In this sense, we would have not only to give up the figure
of height but also the figure of depth, if the depth is taken to be a
ground instead of an abyss.

From the point of view of deconstruction, Tillich has recourse to
a back-up system, a more deeply lodged foundation that he inherits
from Hegel and Schelling (1775–1854, a contemporary and rival
of Hegel), in virtue of which contingent (conditioned, constructed)
things acquire a deeper meaning and steadier purpose. If our constant claim is that it is in the best interests of theology to avoid the
Supreme Being, the high and mighty God, and to drain the cup of
God's weakness and folly, then it is also in our interest to take the
next step, to avoid the relocation of high and mighty discourse to
the realm of the "deep." Tillich's notion of replacing the dynamics of height with depth is revolutionary, but depth must not be
allowed to take over the functions formerly performed by height,
lest the God formerly known as high and mighty reappear, this time
donning the garments of the "ground of being." Too often, I think,
Tillich is doing just that. The being, power, and might of God make
a return appearance in Tillich under the form of a more elemental,
deep-set ground—God, the power of being, God, the depth of
being-itself.[47] Much as I love the depths of Tillich's "depth" dimension, I think it has done all that it can do for us and we now require
an alternative, which I propose is the "event."

I think there is a not well-hidden alliance of Tillich with the old
metaphysical theology of the high and mighty. Revolutionary as he
is—I am trying mightily not to be ungrateful, trying not to kill the
father of radical theology—Tillich is engaged in a shift from a metaphysics of power on high to a metaphysics of power down below.
Tillich's theology ends up being a metaphysical theology, after all,
not of the theistic sort but of the post-theistic sort; not a theism but
a panentheism; and not of the highest being but of the ground of
being. There is a deep onto-centering and even Christo-centering in
Tillich which operates a floor below the offices of classical theology

up above. The result is that all the attributes of God found in the classical and rather Neoplatonic treatises on the divine names of orthodox theology are reinstated in Tillich, and lead to a panentheistic or process metaphysics. Thus the Providence of God is relocated in the meaning of history. The eternity of God is relocated in the everlasting inexhaustibility of time. That is, incidentally, what everlasting meant in the scriptures before the interpretation of scripture fell prey to Greek metaphysics, which is why radical theology is in part a de-Hellenization of God and recalling the Jewishness of God.

## Muting Mystical Theology

So the itinerary of weak theology on the road to freeing God from being is to say: God is not a being; but neither is God the ground or being of beings. But—and this is the next step—neither is God the hyper-being, the *hyperousios* of mystical theology. Apophatic theology is the forbidden fruit in weak theology because a great deal of weak theology sounds just like it—unsaying what we say about God, dethroning language about God that comes off as pretentious. But don't bite. Mystical theology, as much as I love it, as much as I depend upon it, as often as I invoke it, parts company with weak theology on a crucial point, one that could not be more crucial: the God of mystical theology is—alternately—both the highest of the high and the deepest of the deep. So if we speak of God in the highest, mystical theology will un-speak that and say that the God beyond God is higher than any height; and if we speak of the depths of God, mystical theology will unsay that by saying the Godhead of God is deeper than any depth. It has various locutions, all quite brilliant: God is being in a higher way, *eminentiore modo*; or as Meister Eckhart says in his Latin works, God is the *puritas essendi*, meaning both the purity from being and the purity of being, being in its purest, beyond and without being.

These are all so many resourceful and innovative ways to praise and protect the superessential hyper-being of God, to inscribe a zone of absolute respect around God's eminence or depth, to unsay what is said in the name of the excess of the God about whom we speak. But all this unsaying, all this apophasis, is doxological; it is meant as *praise*—to God in the very highest, as the God beyond being, or the Godhead beyond God, or God in the ground of being—and so as a way of ultimately centering our discourse and relieving it of its disorientation. Here silence is praise. *Silentium tibi laus.* But in a theology of the unconditional, when we speak of the groundless, we are not praising anything, and when we are silent, it is because we remain radically disoriented, not knowing which way to turn, not because we are resonating with the mystery of the hyper-being.

To be clear, mystical theology does not adopt the high and mighty discourse of metaphysics. It is not metaphysical in its *how* but in its *what.* It is not metaphysical in its *discursive form*, since it unsays any attempt to form concepts or propositions about God, or to make arguments about the existence of the *hyperousios.* But it is presenting a kind of hyper-metaphysics in *substance*, in *what* it is talking about, the God beyond God to whom it is praying. Mystical theology is not saying that we cannot get as far as metaphysics but that we cannot be content with metaphysics since metaphysics cannot get as far as God. It is not following the line of weakening: it is not saying that God does not get as far as being; it is pursuing the line of eminence and strength, that being does not get as far as God.[48] It is seeking a way to keep God safe from merely metaphysical or objectifying discourse.

That is why, underneath its apophaticism, there almost always lies, big as life (especially in the Christian tradition), some form of Neoplatonism, which was the fundamental philosophical influence on the early Church fathers, both Greek and Latin, and reached its high point in St. Augustine, who influenced everything thereafter. Along with Neoplatonism comes all the metaphysical baggage of the One and the Many, the Eternal and the Temporal, the Sensible and the Supersensible, the body and the soul, being (*ousia*) and beyond being (*hyperousia*). There the Good is beyond being because being is but the first effect of the unutterable Good, a trope that goes back to the medieval *Liber de causis* and ultimately to Plato's *Republic*. This has distorted biblical interpretation and helped (mis)shape classical (strong) theology, which is one of the reasons we needed a Reformation to give Jesus equal time with Greek metaphysics. Mystical theology allows Being in through the back door of apophasis, laced in the garments of a hyper-being.

Mystical theology is, to this extent, not foolish at all, and not the sort of divine folly which we seek. But were we to pursue the question of mystical theology more closely we would go on to show that it also has another voice, a minor chord, in which it exposes itself to a more radically de-centering abyss that lies in foreswearing its deep and centering ground. To proceed further, to venture into an abyss like that, would be more like the folly of God we have in mind. But that is another matter.[49]

In sum, what lies behind Tillich's ground of being is the metaphysics of German Idealism, and what lies behind the mystical theology is the metaphysics of Neoplatonism. In this regard, these are philosophies of being or ultra-being, not the foolishness of God. They undo the unconditionality of the unconditional and they are completely foreign to the coming of the kingdom of God which was announced by "Yeshua," his Aramaic name, which defamiliarizes "Jesus," a name that brings with it infinite baggage.

# 7

# A Theology
# of Perhaps

I hasten to add that freeing God from the order of being also frees
God from a simple declaration of non-being, which belongs to the
same order. The latter might take the form of a flat-out declaration
that God is an illusion, as in psychoanalysis, where the notion that
God is the solution to our problems is held as evidence against God.
Or it might take the form of a disproof of God's existence in the
manner of the so called new atheists, who think that science shows
that God definitely does not exist. Any such proof or disproof as
that is too strong, too overbearing, too much high and mighty
talk. I am not proposing a negative ontological argument, that the
very idea of God makes no sense and that such a being could not
possibly exist. I am not trying to disprove God's existence. I am
trying to repeat what is going on in the name of God in another
way and in another register, the one to which the folly of God
belongs. I am not saying that, once and for all, there is no God,
no Supreme Being. I am simply saying that, with Jean-François
Lyotard (1924–98), the French philosopher who is responsible for
the received definition of post-modernism as "incredulity about
meta-narratives,"[50] I greet the Supreme Being with supreme incredulity. The French expression translated as "meta-narratives" is
"*grands récits*," grand narratives, big stories, tall tales, or what I am
calling here high and mighty discourse. These are strong, overarch-
ing accounts that pretend to give us a theory of everything, to get
to the bottom line, to have a totalizing reach, to reach what Hegel
called "absolute knowledge." Considered thus, atheism is every bit

as much a big story, a metanarrative, a high and mighty discourse as theism. Proofs of the non-existence of God are every bit as much hot air as proofs for God's existence; each would keep the balloons of metaphysics aloft indefinitely.

## Incredulity about the Supreme Being

Lyotard's choice of words is exquisite: incredulity, *in* + *credere*, not believable, which is a wound in the side of every Creed, Nicene or otherwise. The key is that he is not saying definitively false, just not believable. I think that Tillich was saying very much the same thing when he said "half-blasphemous and mythological," an anthropocentric picture card God, a super-agent who does things or sends us into a tizzy when he mysteriously declines doing things that we think really need doing, etc. You can believe all that if you want, and we will not call the police on you, just the way we won't call the police if you believe in alien abductions. It's just that such a belief in a being such as the Supreme Being is making itself more and more unbelievable with every passing day. You can believe it if you want, but the result is fideism, believing something that makes you feel safe, including feeling safe that no one can really prove you wrong. You may think that that the unconditional would have an easier time of it if it had the existence of God to back it up, and you can believe that if you want, it's a free country, but you will buy yourself a host of problems. What problems? I see three big ones.

(1) If there is a Supreme Being up there, the result is to demean everything that is precious in life (unconditional) by inserting it into an economy of rewards and punishments (conditions). We raise children by teaching them the difference between right and wrong, and we do this by means of rewards and punishments. When they behave well we lavish praise, hugs and treats upon them; everybody on the little league team gets a trophy, no matter how humble their contributions. When children misbehave, they are punished, which consists nowadays mostly of "time-outs" (back in the day the

methods were, well, stronger). We do this just so long as and until they grow up, that is, when they internalize these principles and can be counted on to act like adults on their own. The religion of the Supreme Being runs on the same principles, but in religion you do not ever get to quite grow up—the whole of life "in time" is a spiritual childhood lived with the hope of eternal rewards and the fear of eternal punishments. It undermines the possibility of acting *unconditionally*. You should love your neighbor but you will fry if you do not. Eternally. Ouch! Can you imagine a marriage like that? It would make Henry VIII look like a benevolent and loyal spouse. That is why Kant won a prize for defining "Enlightenment" as the human race reaching its maturity and "daring to think" for itself and that is why religion tends not to do so well among the dare-to-think set.

(2) If there is a Supreme Being up there, then he (I am unapologetic about his gender in this case) will be so high and mighty that we will be able to know little or nothing about him unless he reveals himself to us. This he will have to do in a particular time and place, culture and language, say, by revealing himself on the local mountain, or by coming down to earth to pass some time among certain people at a certain time and place, picking out who will be the people of God and creating a barrel of trouble for other people whom he did not pick. This claim to fame, to be the very people of God, the ones to whom the god made a "special" revelation, *our* God, who revealed himself to us (it's always *us*), who will make our enemies our footstool, will fan the flames of confessionalism, of the chosen people, and inevitably—let history be my witness—of religious violence. The author of Psalm 110:1 was not jesting. It will require an enormous expenditure of time and energy and diplomacy to walk all this back, to put out all these fires, and that—let history be my witness—will not succeed. Once again, you are free to believe in such a Supreme Being, but it is more trouble than it's worth.

(3) If there is a Supreme Being up there, an agent capable of creating a cosmic order, of performing miracles and wondrous

works, of intervening on behalf of the persecuted, of stopping the
evil ones in their tracks, then you will have a devil of a time, if I may
put it that way, explaining why the Supreme Being does what he
does, does not do what we fervently hoped he would do, or seems
to be standing by idly, arms folded, watching us go under for the
third time while the evil ones are having a great party up on their
yachts. The record of the Supreme Being of stopping the evil ones
in their tracks, of making our enemies our footstool, of shrinking
cancerous tumors, and the like, is so bad, you have to wonder why
the theologians keep bringing it up. If you think it will require an
enormous expenditure of time and energy to put out the fires of
hell or the fires of confessionalism, that pales in comparison with
the libraries that have been filled trying to resolve the dilemmas of
"theodicy," of the problem of evil. Once again, you are free to place
your credulity in such a Supreme Being, but in addition to all the
anthropocentrism and anthropomorphism, all the mythology and
semi-blasphemy you have on your hands, it is more trouble than
it's worth.

    Of course, I am not the first one to voice those concerns. I am
just saying that Lyotard has put his finger on something that helps
explain their growing force among the dare-to-think set these days.
Religion, with its unrelenting supernaturalism and mythologizing,
is making itself more and more unbelievable and is seeing to it that
belief flourishes best among the most deprived and desperate, the
poorest and most undereducated people on the globe, while finding itself increasingly irrelevant to everyone else. We are fast approaching the point where once an individual or a culture reaches a
certain stage of intellectual clarity and economic stability, even after
centuries of doctrinal servitude, its religious beliefs become, well,
unbelievable and incur mass incredulity. Contemporary Ireland is
the most recent example but the same thing is beginning to happen
among the growing middle class in South America.

    My focus in all three concerns, but especially in the first, which
I will emphasize here, is that the unconditionality of the uncondi-

tional is undermined or short-circuited once the unconditional is identified as God. Or, I hasten to add, as anything else—as Humanity or Nature, as Science or Spirit, as the Nation or the Party, or whatever! I will come back to this in my discussion of the dynamics of the call coming up next (chapter 8). Suffice it for the moment to say that, in weak or radical theology, we do not seek to disprove the existence of a Supreme Being; we just greet it with the sustained incredulity it has earned for itself. Incredulity is its just deserts. Ultimately, I will contend, this High and Mighty One, this God, would be the undoing of the kingdom of God (chapter 10).

## A Theology of Perhaps

So will nothing satisfy us? If God is neither a highest being, nor being itself, nor a mystical beyond being, and if we are not trying to prove God's outright non-being, if none of this will do, what is there left for weak theology to do? The short answer is I never promised a rose garden. The longer answer is the unconditional, but I never said the unconditional is not demanding business! The clue lies in the link between the unconditional and the folly of God that I have been following, which shows up in the difference between the language used by Tillich and Derrida. Tillich sometimes speaks of the Uncondition*ed, das Unbedingte,* meaning something enjoying the ontological status of being or of the ground of being, whereas Derrida always speaks of the "unconditional*,*" meaning something without being. Whenever Derrida speaks of the unconditionals, like justice, he will add "perhaps" (*peut-être*), or "if there is any," "if there is such a thing" (*s'il y en a*), which of course—if it is genuinely undeconstructible—there is not. Were any such thing as justice to exist, were justice an existing thing, an existent, an entity, it would be a construction, an effect of the system of differences, and as such deconstructible, and then justice would not be undeconstructible, unconditional. When we embrace the madness that makes everything turn on something we are not at all sure is there, or how it is there, or exactly what it means or does, then we are in

closest proximity to the genuine folly of God, which Paul tells us
stands by the things that are not to shame the things that are. The
folly of Derrida's unconditional is closely linked to this "perhaps."

But what then, "is" an unconditional for Derrida? The first thing
to say, of course, is that whatever it is, it is not a "what" and "is"
is an inappropriate thing to say about it—which is why Derrida so
often calls upon the semantic and linguistic resources of negative
theology. The best thing to say is that the unconditional does not
exist; it insists. The folly of the unconditional is not to exist. The
unconditional calls, lures, solicits, provokes, spooks, and haunts—
but it does not have the good sense to exist, so do not rush to the
conclusion that there is a reassuring entity up there or down here
which does the calling, luring, spooking, etc. In addition to avoid-
ing the hypostatization, the personification, the mythologization,
we must also avoid the ontologization. The folly of God is that God
does not exist. God insists, but God does not exist. So steer clear
of the interminable and bombastic wars between the theists and the
atheists and pay quiet heed to the phenomenon, to the event, to the
unconditional, as maddeningly elusive as it may be. That is why I
say we should stick to the middle voice, and always say that a call is
*getting itself called in* the traditions and languages we inherit. That,
I propose, is a postmodern counter-part to Augustine speaking of
finding God *in memoria*. We wake up one day in the middle of the
world and find that language is already running, that our *memoria*
is already well stocked in advance with promises and memories, calls
and recalls, hopes and fears that we have inherited. We start from
where we are, where we first find ourselves, undertaking that life-
long negotiation between the conditional and the unconditional,
which we call the story of our lives.

The unconditional is a homeless, uncanny sort of thing or nothing that does not inhabit the house of being. It is not the subject
matter of a panentheistic metaphysics (which we distinguished
from "pantheism" back in chapter 1). It is not God's life on earth
as the Absolute Spirit (Hegel) but rather something more spectral

that gives us no peace. It is not Divine Providence transcribed into space and time but a more radical roll of the dice, a promise/threat, where the risk runs all the way down, where the folly is to follow the risk all the way without turning back. The unconditional is not inserted within a reassuring dialectic of finite and infinite such that the infinite is working itself out in finite ways. The unconditional in Derrida is not infinite being, not being itself, not the being of beings, not a hyper-being, but something otherwise and elsewhere, an infinitival in-finite, a to-come, a messianic promise (without a Messiah), a figure of hope against hope—how foolish is that?—in the coming of something that we cannot see coming, which may turn out to be a disaster. If the unconditional is a possibility resonating in the present, the stirring of an event, it is so only as the coming of the unforeseeable, a memory of the immemorial. The unconditional is not merely a means of admitting our frailty, fallibility, and finitude in the face of the infinite; it is a more radical confession or circumfession that the unforeseeability of the future, the coming of what we cannot see coming, goes all the way down, overtaking God as well as us, which is where the folly is found.

Above and beyond all else (to adopt a high flying trope I am otherwise trying to avoid), the difference which makes all the difference between Tillich's Unconditioned and Derrida's unconditional, has to do with the death of God. For Tillich God is inexhaustible being, and so the strictly, deeply theological "atheism" he advocated could never become—although this is precisely what did become of it in the 1960s—the "death of God." The death of God for Tillich (not for the post-Tillichians) would be an absurdity, a contradiction in terms. Death reaches as far as individual finite beings, but it cannot lay a glove on the infinite, inexhaustible ground of being. Non-being can never overtake being itself; death can never reach as far as life itself. Individual beings are born and die, but not being itself. Death has no power over the power and ground of being. But for Derrida the unconditional means that what lies ahead is a chance for life, a hope against hope, a desire beyond desire. But it may very

well be a catastrophe, a disaster, death and destruction, the death
of God and of the human, a crucifixion of both God and humanity.
It just might be that what is coming spells the end of God, that the
coming God will be stillborn. The coming of what we cannot see
coming might be the death not simply of individual living things
but of life itself in a solar expansion which will turn the earth to
toast, or a coming cosmic destruction, an irreversible entropic dissipation which will be the end of all ends, the death of death, the
death of the cycle of life-and-death itself.

Maybe. Perhaps. *Peut-être.*[51]

In weak theology, the might of God Almighty is weakened into
might-be, and the being of the Supreme Being is weakened into
may-being (from *être* to *peut-être*). The folly of God is that the
name (of) "God" is not the name of the Supreme Being, or the
ground of being, or the mystical Hyper-being, but of may-being,
of "perhaps," of the event of what is calling and being called for, of
the possibility of the impossible, which may perhaps be a disaster.
By this I do not mean that God may exist but we just do not know,
and so, not being sure, it is wiser to withhold judgment and to be
evasive if anyone presses us for an answer. The folly of God means
instead that the event contained in the name of God is the event
of the "maybe," of the "perhaps," of what Nietzsche called the
"dangerous" perhaps, since every promise is a threat. In speaking
of "perhaps" I do not align myself with indifference, neutrality, and
indecisiveness. I am not in search of a way to evade commitment,
to safely sit on the fence between theism and atheism, to say I just
don't know. My perhaps does not imply the paralysis of skepticism.
The perhaps of which I speak really is dangerous because it pushes
us out into the cold, exposes us to the unforeseeable, leaving us
unprotected, at risk, full of hope and so also exposed to despair. By
perhaps I mean to pursue the tracks of the unknown, which may be,
perhaps, a monster. To tangle with this perhaps is pure folly.

"When they say, 'There is peace and security', then sudden
destruction will come upon them, as labor pains come upon a

pregnant woman, and there will be no escape!" (1 Thess 5:3). My perhaps is like that. When things seem safe and settled and secure, my perhaps intervenes and upsets everything by insinuating, "perhaps not." I am saying the folly of the name of God signals something about our lives. This name whispers in our ears that we live in response to the promptings of a distant promise, to the solicitude of a spirit or specter little known, to a real beyond the real. It requires us to cultivate what Keats called a negative capability, a capacity to sustain uncertainty and to live a life of folly.

The event contained in the name (of) "God" exceeds calculation, evades rules, eludes any program. The name of God is the name of the chance of an event. The kingdom of God is the name of the realm where the event pays a unexpected call upon us, waking us in the middle of the night with a loud rapping at our door.

# 8

# The Folly
# of the Call

The folly of God is that God does not exist; God insists. God does not exist; God calls. God's folly is that, not thinking existence something to cling to, God emptied himself into the world (Phil 2: 6–7), leaving existence to us, which is risky business, both for God and for us, since we may or may not follow through. The insistence of God means that the name of God is not the name of a Supreme Being, but the name of a call, to which we may or may not respond. The name of God is the name of something unconditional that makes an unexpected call upon us in the night. How so?

## God's Promise

I have said several times that as soon as we wake up in the world we find that language is already running. Language, like the world, started without us. As we said earlier (chapter 2), when we wake up in the world we find ourselves in the midst of multiple ongoing systems or matrices that generate the relatively stable unities of meaning that make up a relatively stable—and therefore relatively unstable or deconstructible—world. These multiple systems are summarized by Derrida with the neologism *différance*, a word he coined in the debate with the Structuralists about the make-up of language. Language is at the forefront of such systems, and it was the test case of choice, but language is far from the only such system. Language is a network that is seamlessly woven into other networks—political, social, historical, religious, cultural, geographical, embodied, gendered, affective, etc. "*Et cetera*" is a bail-out phrase meaning such systems go on and on and it would be impossible to spell them all out. If I leave one out, and my critics bring it up in the reviews, I will say with a smirk that that is what I meant by "etc." Whatever else they are, these systems make up our legacy, or inheritance, our postmodern Augustinian *memoria*, a body of background structures that invisibly shape our lives. They include the beliefs and practices, the institutions and the traditions we inherit, all the systems that are already running. They include precious deposits that we moderns call our "values" and that the ancients called "wisdom" (*sophia*), the good, the true and the beautiful, which we pursue (*philia*). These deposits, I am claiming, are both promises and memories of things in which our desires, or what Augustine called the restlessness of our hearts, are concentrated.

One of the examples of an unconditional, and it was far from just an example, to which Derrida returned again and again, is "democracy." That is all at once an inherited memory, a legacy, that goes back to the proto-democratic institutions of ancient Athens; a present reality in the variously democratic institutions to be found in contemporary life; and a promise that has not yet been kept, not quite. I say a promise because every existing democracy is subject to the Protestant-Jewish principle: no conditioned, existing entity is ever equal to the demands of the unconditional; no existing democracy is ever a match for the democracy-to-come; no existing democracy fulfills the promise of democracy, which is why we could say, as foolish as it may sound, "my fellow democrats, there are no democrats."[52] All of this is to say that there is no democracy that responds to all that is called for and recalled in democracy. What is democracy? However you might define it in a given place or time, democracy is a call in which something—let's say both freedom and equality—is being called for and getting itself called. It is a call for something unconditional to which no existing response is adequate. Any existing democratic state or institution is a conditioned response to an unconditional call made under the particular conditions of space and time, history and culture, in which it finds itself. So true is this that if anything like what is being called for un-conditionally in and under this name ever showed up, it might not even be called "democracy," which is why we do not want to call the unconditional an "ideal," as if we know where we are going but we just have been unable so far to get there. So, to generalize, what is being called for are the various hopes and desires that are depos-ited in the traditions that we inherit, in words of elemental promise lodged in those traditions. These words express the multiple hopes and desires that we want to keep as open-ended as possible so as not to block their future, lest we prevent the event and close off the incoming of what is coming. As a legacy, what is being called for is also the recalling of what has been calling to us all along, from of old, from time immemorial. Democracy is but one of them. Their name is legion. There are thousands of them—like justice, love, friendship, mercy, life, all to come.

For some of us, at least, this list would include the promise of theology and of God, of a theology-to-come, a coming generation of theologians dedicated to thinking a coming God, a God-to-come, one that is lodged deep *in memoria* and is also far off as a distant lure. That is why I am constantly reworking, rephrasing, redoing, repolishing, revising, reediting, refining, and qualifying my language by speaking not simply about God but about the event that takes place in the name (of) "God." I am saying that—for some of us at least—the name (of) "God" is a kind of concen-tration or constellation, a composition or compilation, of these promises and memories, all gathered up into one word. The name (of) "God" is symbolic and metaphoric, but also metonymic of the whole constellation. That puts unbearable pressure on this or any one finite empirical word, which is when and why we have recourse to apophatic discourse. I venture the hypothesis, tentatively and full of fear and trembling, that this constellation of metaphors and metonyms—which go to make up what I will shortly call a "poet-ics" (chapter 9)—is itself organized around the leading trope of the "possibility of the impossible," the search for the impossible representing, of course, the height or depth of folly. This I treat as a focal desire, what I might also venture to call the very structure of desire, of a desire beyond desire, which means the structure is also de-structuring. By this I mean that we desire with a desire not contained within our horizon of expectation, like aspiring to graduate *summa cum laude* or to rise to the presidency of the company. I mean a desire beyond the foreseeable, a desire for the unforeseeable, which (I always add) is risky business, which means it is folly to fool around with it. It takes a certain amount of audacity, maybe even madness, to call for the coming of what you cannot see coming! You never know what to expect next. But I think that God, that the name of God, that the folly (of) "God," is the paradigmatic name of that desire—given certain conditions!

So the name of God is not the name of a Supreme Being, or of the ground of being, or of a Hyper-being. It is the name of an event, of the call of an event, of the event of a call. I do not seek to displace the Supreme Being with the "ground of being" but with the event. I refigure the figure and the concept of "ground" with the notion of *what is going on* in and under these inherited names. My question always is: *What is going on* when classical theology speaks of a Supreme Being, or when Tillich speaks of the ground of being, or when the mystics speak of a Hyper-being or when piety says "my God"? The answer is the event. What is *being called for* in and under the name of God? The answer is the possibility of the impossible, the possibility of the event. The question of what we call in Christian Latin English religion is always how to speak of the element in which we live and move and have our being. The answer is the coming of the event, the call for the coming of what we cannot see coming, of what eye has not seen nor ear heard, what has not entered into the minds of human beings. That is why lotteries are sure to make money. In uttering the name of God we expose the horizons of our lives to the impossible, to thinking what we cannot think, to imagining the unimaginable, to speaking what cannot be said, with a hope against hope, with a faith that moves mountains, with a love that outlasts death. The name of God names a passage to the limit, to an excess, to something unconditional, and leads to a divine madness.

## The Folly of the Call

As Heidegger shows us in a couple of masterful sections from *Being and Time*, of any call we must ask three things: Who or what is being called upon? Who or what is being called for? Who or what is calling?[53]

1. As we have set out to find what the interest of theology is, and what is in the best interests of theology, and as theology is something we ourselves are doing, then it is clear that we ourselves are the ones (the beings or entities) who are *called upon*. What is being called for in and under the name of God is "on us," in the accusative. We are the ones under the gun, being asked to respond. We are the ones God has been waiting for.

2. What is *being called for* is the realization of these promises that are being made in the traditions and institutions we have inherited, or of the memories that are being recalled, that come to us from time immemorial. What is being called for is to do the impossible, as far as that is possible; to go where we cannot go, as far as we can; to make the unconditionals come true under concrete conditions; to construct the undeconstructible, which of course is impossible.

3. But it is the third question I want to pause over here. If we ask who or what is calling, the answer should be straightforward: God. In theology, we are talking about the word of God, literally, trying to put our finger on the *logos* of *theos*. The various and variously religious traditions are so many different responses to which God is the call. But if we have learned anything so far it is that things are never straightforward with God—with the name (of) "God." That name is first of all part of that legacy or inheritance or tradition which is already

running when we wake up in the world, a word that many of us first learned from our mother's lips, back in the beginnings of our lives, in a time out of mind. (Unless we did not.) The name (of) "God" is an effect of these matrices or systems of difference, one among many of the relatively stable (and so unstable) unities of meaning that are produced by these multiple systems nicknamed *différance*.

But it might have been otherwise. We might have had a different childhood, lived in an altogether different time and place and world, might have heard this name as the emblem of everything irredeemably evil, of everything repressive and regressive. We might never have heard this word at all or we might have heard it quite differently, where it is not so high and mighty, and does not occur in the singular. It may not even be found at all, which is to say, a careful inquiry into a very different culture would show that there is no more or less fixed equivalent to what "we" call God. When I say "we" who do I mean? I am referring to those of us who live in and among the great monotheistic traditions, the religions of the Book. It is there that the name (of) "God," capitalized and in the singular, serves as the name of our desire beyond desire for what is unconditional in our lives, for what calls upon us unconditionally to transform our lives.

So a certain indefiniteness, ambiguity, and non-knowing descends over the question of who or what is calling (and it belongs to a theology of the unconditional to maintain the unconditional in this indefinite mode and thereby to keep it safe). Are these traditions the bearer of the word of God who has revealed Godself in the world? Are they the result of an intervention into history by the Supreme Being (classical theism)? Or the way that the ground of being emerges into the various cultural forms of life that make up history (Tillich)? Or a merely contingent name for the nameless and eternal One or Good beyond being (mystical theology)? Who knows that? If we knew that, we would know everything. All we do know is that when we woke up in the world this name and the systems or matrices of systems to which it belongs were already running. My hypothesis is that what makes this name run, what makes it special, what sustains it—apart from a lot of violence—is that it is the name of the possibility of the impossible, while remaining in the weak mode of an unconditional call. Consequently, it is the name, or one of the names, we have for pushing our lives to the limit, for keeping these systems open ended and exposed to the future. Otherwise, instead of being inspired by them we will expire; they will suffocate us and we will give up the ghost. These systems have a vacant center, a central void that is never filled in, a gap that is never closed, a future that is always coming. They represent the gap God opens, not the gap God fills.

That is why I keep the call in the middle voice, and speak of what is being called, what is getting itself called, in the call. So when I say the caller of the call is indefinite, I am not withholding something, not trying to keep a secret, not trying to keep my cards close to my chest and conceal what I really think. I am not even complaining. I am not saying that with a little more research and better data and a little bit of luck and access to better computers we hope eventually to track down the source, to identify the caller, to spell it all out. I am saying that the caller of the call is indefinite *as a structural matter*, in principle, and that it is *better* that way, that the Protestant-Jewish principle concedes that we are finite, conditioned creatures, that is, wounded and exposed to something I know not what. This is a secret, but it is not a secret I am keeping but a secret that is being kept, in the middle voice. It is a *structural* secret and it is the task of a theology of the unconditional to maintain and protect this secret. The folly of the call lies in the secret, in the non-knowing, where the non-knowing is not a defect but constitutive of it in a positive way, just the way that what we do not know in science drives science on, just the way the secret innermost thoughts of the other person are irreducibly constitutive in a positive way of their being another person. If we knew what others were thinking, if we knew their secret, then their otherness, what they call in postmodern theory their "alterity," would be abolished. Not only would all hell break loose—it would be worse than having all our email published on-line—but our experience of the other, what we have to learn from others, what we enjoy in our encounters, everything that makes them other, every surprise of which they are capable, would be abolished. The event that is contained in the name of God is like that. If we knew it was God who was calling, it could not possibly be what is going on in the name of God, for that would shrink the folly of God down into knowledge. That would be God's foil, not God's folly.

Heidegger says that the call has a quiet and unsettling anonymity about it, such that we are deprived of saying who calls and what is being called for.[54] If pressed about the matter, the best we can do is to say "it calls," that something is getting itself called, with what Heidegger calls all the "uncanniness" of an "it." The word uncanny suggests something spooky, so that to say "it calls" is also to say "it spooks." The call not only calls for the coming of what we cannot see coming; the call itself seems to come from nowhere, at least nowhere that we can locate, uninvited and from no one whom we can identify, and in a very real sense it tells us nothing, gives us no information, does not communicate anything in particular. All we can say is that it calls, it happens, it summons us, it calls us to account, it stops us in our tracks, it gets our attention—and it is up to us to make something happen in return. It may very well do all this in the mode of keeping silent, Heidegger adds. In a quiet moment, when we are lost for words, struck dumb, simply brought up short. It may be that it can only be heard when there is nothing to hear, in the midst of a very crushing silence, when words fail us.

Where is this call coming from? Is it from God? From the ground of being? From our inherited culture? Our DNA? Some dark cosmic force? Is it a bit of a disturbance in our bones caused by dark matter? Is it anything more than a bit of undigested beef, as Nietzsche so mercilessly asks? Who knows? As Heidegger says, "If the caller is asked about its name, status, origin, or repute, it not only refuses to answer, but does not even leave the slightest possibility of one's making it into something with which one can be familiar."[55] The caller holds itself aloof, and this, Heidegger says, is "distinctive for it in a *positive* way," because if it were identifiable, the whole thing would be undermined, like knowing the thoughts of other persons. If we could identify the caller, assess the credentials of the source, evaluate its authority, we would get on top of it, make it our own. The call would come in on an ontological caller ID. We would get out of the accusative into the nominative, convert it into one of *my* possibilities, something I am doing on my own. If I could say this is God or biology or culture, there would be an end to it. My mind would be put at ease. It would become my idea and were I to respond to it after some deliberation, I would be doing what I want and think best. I would be back at the wheel, going where I want to go, not where I am called. Then it would be my call and that would undermine my being called, in the accusative, my being summoned to act unconditionally, against my expectations, against my inclinations, from beyond me. That would deprive the call of its uncanniness, of its riskiness, of its madness and folly.

The Viennese shrink (Freud)—or he may be a sarcastic French fellow (Lacan)—sitting behind the couch, stroking his beard, listens to all this patiently, hearing me out to the end (he is paid by the hour even if he cuts the session short). Having been particularly alarmed when I mentioned being spooked, he begins to explain to me that there are no spooks and that this is what they call in his trade a projection. But allow me to insist (he calls this being in denial): this is not some projection of mine but the result of my having been ejected or thrown into a world that is already running. This is something to which I have always already been delivered over, as Heidegger puts it, from the first time I opened my eyes. It is not a projection but a projectile. It is not in my head but coming at my head. It is calling to me—I am not involved in an inner soliloquy. If I were in charge, I would shut it down at once. Who wants to be spooked like this? Who wants to be made a fool? For the most part, I would just as soon forget it, manage not to notice it, wait for it to go away, go on a cruise and hope that it is gone when I come home. This is definitely not my doing; it is the last thing I would do. This is running without me.

If we could get on top of what calls upon us unconditionally, we would undermine its unconditionality, just the way knowing the caller enables us to decide whether we want to answer the telephone. We would end up entering the unconditional into one or another conditioned order, inserting it in one or another order of conditioned effects whose names we do know—it is the call of God, the Nation, the Party, Nature, our Neurophysiology. If I were ever to succumb to a high and mighty discourse, if I were just once to indulge myself like that, I would say that we weak theologians have been sent into the world—this is our world-historical mission—in order to save the call, to protect its sources, to secret away its secretiveness. We have been called into the world in the name of the call and have been commissioned, sent out two by two, with just a staff and no knapsack, to protect the anonymity of the call, to surround and keep safe its unknowability, to keep its folly safe. That is why weak theology looks so much like apophatic theology, which in a certain way it is—*without* all the Neoplatonic hype about the *hyperousios* and the eternal still Godhead beyond God, or the deep metaphysics of German Idealism. We must keep the call weak, not let it get puffed up, not let it grow strong and loud and bombastic. It calls, something is getting itself called for, in all its uncanniness and anonymity, where all that matters is its being heard, our being summoned, our response. The only worldly testimony to this other-worldly (spooky) call is our response. It insists; we exist. The existence of our response is the only way the insistence of the call acquires existence or makes an appearance in the world. For all the world, to everyone else in the world, we are dancing to music they do not hear, which makes us look like fools.

# 9

# Mustard Seeds
# Not Metaphysics

## The Theopoetics of the Kingdom of God

Before we move on to the question that I posed at the start, "Does the kingdom of God need God?," I need to add one more piece to the puzzle, which concerns the nature of theology as a discourse. Here the logic of the unconditional, which is a logic of weakening, takes the next step, which is to let theo*logy* weaken into what I will describe here under the name of a theo*poetics*. It is of no little importance to identify the discursive type of a "gospel" if we are to understand what someone is doing who shows up one day and announces good news to the poor, release for the imprisoned, sight for the blind, freedom for the oppressed, and the year of the Jubilee (Luke 4:16–21), that is, the coming rule of God. I claim that the discourse on the kingdom of God proclaimed in the gospels takes the form of a poetics which theology itself accordingly is duty bound to observe. In the next and concluding section (chapter 10), I hope finally to find the courage to face up to the full force of the folly I am caught up in by facing up to the full brunt of the question, does the kingdom of God need God?

## Theopoetics

In weak theology, the word theology itself is too strong. So the voice of theology must be softened, allowed to weaken from a *logos* of God, the logic of the Supreme Being, into a *poetics* of the event that is taking place in the name (of) "God." Let me say here at the

93

start that by a poetics I mean a collection of metaphors, metonyms, narratives, allegories, songs, poems, and parables, indeed an assembling of *all* the rhetorical strategies we can summon, in order to address the event. The idea is not so much to expound the event as to allow ourselves to be exposed to the event, to let it come and to let ourselves come under its sway. In theopoetics, we are not trying to propose propositions that represent a state of affairs, but to let the event happen and to let it happen to us. I put this by saying we let strong theology weaken into the softer, gentler tones of theopoetics, which is best explained by contrasting theopoetics with theology.

The classical sense of theology, which is a word taken from Aristotle to signify a cool-handed science (*episteme, scientia*) of being at its best, of the true being (*to on*) or substance (*ousia*) of the highest being, is to put its finger on the *logos* of that being. A theology is tasked with coming up with a set of concepts, propositions, and arguments that do their best to figure out the being of the best and the brightest, of the god (*theos*). That being, Aristotle famously concluded, is a pure form circulating in the sky which dedicates its imperishable substance to thinking the thought of its changeless self while giving sublunaries like ourselves no thought at all.[56] Such a perfect being does not suffer sinners gladly. In fact, it never heard of sinners and does not suffer at all. It is impervious to change and utterly unmindful of us or anything else other than itself, all of which are both figuratively and literally, both ontologically and cosmologically, beneath it. The formidable challenge that faced Thomas Aquinas and later on Hegel was to somehow sync that Aristotelian pure act with the one whom Jesus called *abba*, who counts our every tear and is moved by our prayers. Luther famously begged off that challenge and simply said that Aristotle had been sent into the world as a punishment for our sins. So "theology" is a word that at the very least should be greeted with some incredulity and raised eyebrows by readers of the gospels.

Theo*poetics* is incredulity about theo*logy*. It is the end of strong theology and the beginning of a weak one. The gospels are a first order theopoetics—narratives, parables, striking sayings, etc.—theo-poetics in practice or at work; weak theology is the second order articulation of theopoetics, which faithfully observes its theopoetic form and avoids going higher, ever mindful of the warning of Dae-dalus. Theology seeks to figure out God as best it can. Theopoetics seeks to find a figurative means to express what is happening to us under the name of God. What is happening is in fact what is meant by the "kingdom of God," that is, what happens when God rules, what the world looks like when it is ruled by God and not by the powers and principalities. So a theopoetics does not mean to figure out the logos but to figure forth the event that is harbored in the name (of) "God." That means that whenever we use the word logos in theopoetics, it is spoken with a certain irony, as when Paul speaks of the "logos of the cross," which is a puzzle to the Greek phi-losophers and perfect foolishness and nonsense to the people in the business of conducting crucifixions. We have to appreciate the huge paradox packed into that phrase, which expresses a very consider-able incredulity about what counts as a logos in the world. It was meant to get in the face of people who put their faith in coming up with a logos in a strong sense, that is, the philosophers at Corinth. (What John means by logos is another matter.)

A theopoetics is a discourse tailored to the unconditional, cut to fit the event that takes place in the name (of) "God." The event is not a garden variety logos. It is neither a being whose existence is to be established, nor an essence whose properties are to be identified, nor a presence whose prestige should intimidate us. The event is a bit of folly, the promise of something coming, where every promise also carries with it a threat. The event is the prospect of something to-come that will shatter the horizons of the present, challenge the prestige of the present, unnerve the powers that be with the spooky prospect that things could be otherwise. The event is not an *ens realissimum*, the realest being of them all; the event does not exist, it insists. The event is not an *ens necessarium*, not a necessary being but the possibility of the impossible. The event is not an *ens supremum*, a high and sovereign being that rules over everything with infinite power. The event is the call paid upon us by the un-conditional but without force, where the folly of the unconditional is to be at best a weak force without an army or big being to back it up. A gospel is a piece of good news announcing the coming of the event and how different it would be were the world to make itself susceptible to the sway of the event. Perhaps.

## Hegel's *Vorstellung*

Historically, Hegel is the turning point for theopoetics. Hegel made the first great breakthrough, but he did not finish what he started, because his theopoetics was a transitional stage that ultimately suc-cumbed to Aristotle's theology. The spell of Aristotle's self-thinking thought was the key to Hegel's rendering of the gospel. So Hegel opened the door to theopoetics, but only half way. Still, if Tillich is the father of radical theology, Hegel is its grandfather. If Tillich put the torch to supernaturalism, it was because Hegel had started the fire. Hegel was not the first but he was the most important and influential thinker to talk us down from the heights of the Supreme Being, to show us how to get on top of God in the highest. When Tillich labeled the Supreme Being, the high and mighty God of re-ligion, a "half-blasphemous and mythological" construction, an idol from which a theological atheism frees us, and when he said that a religious language about God is "symbolic," Tillich had Hegel and Schelling, whose later lectures were attended by Kierkegaard, in the back of his mind. That paved the way forward to postmodern theology.

The central move that Hegel made to weaken the high and mighty God of classical theology was to say that the standard re-ligious conception of God as the Supreme Being, as a powerful agent, a doer of miraculous deeds, is what he called a *Vorstellung*.

The standard translation of this word is "representation," which I have described above as a kind of picture post card, a pictorial presentation, depicting something deeper. In speaking of religion this way Hegel was not behaving like an Enlightenment critic trying to knock religion down. His idea of a *Vorstellung* was not meant to raze religion but to *re*think it in a sympathetic, albeit symbolic and revolutionary way. Religion is not false, Hegel maintained. It is not an illusion. It is just a little green, still somewhat untrue, not quite the mature, developed, whole truth, not quite ready for the prime time of first philosophy. To the extent that it exists, religion must be true, otherwise it would not exist at all. But in religion being and truth have not yet ripened, not yet hit full stride.[57] A religious revelation, Hegel said, is a revelation of the truth, but it is not—and this is how it is described while we are still in the pictorial mode—an unveiling made by a Supreme Being of truths too high for mortals down below to reach. A religion contains a revelation, and a revelation is an eye-opener, a new disclosure of the world, a new vision. But religion does this in an imaginative mode, painting a picture-story of the truth, taking the form of narratives, striking sayings, and dramatic scenes that make for riveting films—like summer blockbusters or animated films portraying the exploits of super-heroes—like the Almighty parting the waters of the sea. To that extent, religion is like a poem, but it is not purely a poem because it is driving home the truth in a deeper way than a work of art. Religion gets closer to the core of the truth than does art. Religion pictures the absolute truth to which it gives imaginative form. Nowadays we might think of a Discovery channel animation of the theory of the Big Bang, which is trying to picture the theory but without the mathematics, where Hegel will supply (the equivalent of) the mathematics, as opposed to an animated film concerned only with entertaining visual effects.

Considering the politics of an established Christian state like nineteenth-century Prussia, Hegel had to couch all this with some diplomacy. Religion, he said, is the absolute truth—which was

greeted with nodding heads at the Ministry of Religious Affairs—
but in the form of a *Vorstellung* (hoping the Minister's attention
had by then moved on to other and more pressing affairs). The
critical move made by Hegel was this. Classical theology turned on
a *regional* distinction between the domains of the natural and the
supernatural—thus far reason and the rest is faith—which Hegel displaced. The traditional distinction was between "rational theology,"
the demonstrable matters attainable by human reason down below,
and "sacred theology," the supernatural matters of faith revealed
from on high by a Supreme Being up above. The philosophers were
admitted into the vestibule of natural theology, but they were to
keep their rationalistic hands off the sanctuary of sacred theology.

Hegel defied that ban. By treating religion as a pictorial representation (*Vorstellung*) of the absolute truth, Hegel demystified or
demythologized the classical idea of sacred theology, which for him
was in the best interests of religion and philosophy. He realized that
all the nourishing meat in theology was contained in the "sacred
theology"—above all in the Trinity and the Incarnation—and that
the rest was mostly gristle and bones, arid rationalism. Confronted
by the Trinity, he says, the Enlightenment philosophers, blinking
their eyes, count on their fingers one-two-three, like men who
cannot get their heads around a metaphor and persist in taking it
literally! But for him, everything depends on gaining access to revelation for thought—not rationalistic Enlightenment logic-chopping
thought, which he called "understanding" (*Verstand*), but a more
sensitive, sweeping and synthesizing kind of thought, which he
called "reason" (*Vernunft*). So Hegel proposed a radically different
kind of distinction: not different regions, natural (here below) and
supernatural (up above), but different *stages* or modalities of the
very *same* thing, different states or degrees of intensity of one and
the same reality, like the liquid, solid, and gaseous states of the same
substance, all of which belonged to the purview of a more ample
and inclusive kind of thought.[58]

In classical theology there are two worlds, one in space and time and the other in eternity. In Hegel, there is only one world, but it manifests itself in different and gradually more intensive stages. The totality of what there is, he called the Absolute Spirit. There is only one world, only one Absolute Spirit, but it manifests itself in varying degrees of clarity, three to be exact. Like the Trinity, of which his philosophy is the loyal image, everything in Hegel's thought comes in threes. In the sphere of the Absolute Spirit, that means art, religion and philosophy. Religious revelation happens in the middle, as a *Vorstellung*. In religion, the Spirit reveals itself to us in a pictorial figure that is more spiritual than art but more sensuous than philosophy. To say religion is a *Vorstellung* is to say it is a work of the pictorial imagination—of its images, stories, and liturgies, which stir up our feeling of solidarity with the Absolute Spirit—but it also has spiritual or intellectual content; it lights up our lives. Religion, which is the "Sabbath" of life, giving the hustle and bustle of daily life an hour of peace and rest, is telling us the meaning of the world and the story of our life. A work of art, by contrast, is more immersed in sensuousness and can only intimate spiritual meaning obliquely and leaves the Spirit in a more implicit state, while philosophy is purely conceptual and conveys the Spirit directly and properly.

Take the example of Christianity, which is really a paradigm for Hegel, not just an example, because Christianity is religion at its best, the "consummate" religion, the complete revelation, to which all the other religions are a precursor. In Christianity, the Eternal Logos (now we mean John's glorious logos, not Paul's crucified logos), preexisting from all eternity and dwelling in another sphere above the heavens, comes down into space and time, is born of a virgin, laid in a manger, kept warm by the breathing of the animals, while angels from on high sing alleluia to God in the highest. This is the greatest *Vorstellung* of them all, a story both deep and sublime, the story of stories, the truest story ever told. No wonder it has

made a fortune for Hallmark cards and department stores all over
Christendom, where it has fueled a season of gift-giving and good
cheer, which everyone enjoys. Hegel is not mocking this story or
Christmas cheer, not one bit. This story is not to be taken lightly
because it really is the absolute truth—in the form of a story. It is
the Unconditional delivered under the conditions of a story. Furthermore, a *Vorstellung* like this, a story, is the *only* form in which
*most* people can absorb the absolute unconditional truth. Religion is
all the truth ordinary people can take in about the Absolute Spirit.
Religion is philosophy for the people, somewhat in the way that
today, for people whose minds are absorbed by sports and who have
never seen the inside of the local Art Museum, sports is the way they
get their art, their experience of the beauty of form and motion, and
maybe their religion, too, given the fervor of fans for their teams,
which is a kind of religious fanaticism.

## Metaphysics Not
## Mustard Seeds

But as a *Vorstellung* religion requires going further; it requires
*thought*, thinking religion through more deeply, figuring out what
is being said in and by religious figures. So if Hegel is not mocking religion, neither does he stop there. Keep digging, and think
through what religion is trying to tell us in its own pictorial and
easily accessible way. Dare to think, just as the Enlightenment
counseled, but do not confuse thinking with the narrow and ham-
fisted logic-chopping simulacrum of thought served up in the
Enlightenment and its off-with-their-heads critique of religion.
Think religion through, but with sensitivity to *what is going on in*
religion. I put these words in italics because this is the language in
which I introduced a theology of the "event," where we distinguish
between a phenomenon and *what is going on in* a phenomenon.
That is the crux of what is revolutionary about Hegel. The Trinity
and the Incarnation are the proper subject matter of philosophy,

indeed its most important material, *but*—and everything turns on this "but"—the philosophers must ask themselves what is going on in these and all the "doctrines" of "revelation."

For Hegel, what *is* always going on is what he called the unfolding life of the Absolute Spirit, which is not unlike what Tillich called the "ground of being," the deep underlying substance of reality, which is working itself out, "revealing" and manifesting itself in art, religion and philosophy. For those who have the training and who are up to it intellectually, there is a deeper unabridged version of the story in the original language, a deeper rendering of it, in which the Absolute Spirit presents itself absolutely, in its full conceptual clarity. There is an unconditional version of the unconditional. And for that we need Aristotle, who was a philosopher, not Jesus, who was a poet. We need metaphysics, not mustard seeds. The self-thinking thought is what thought thinks when it thinks religion through.

But to the ancient Greek Aristotle, the German Christian Lutheran Hegel adds the Incarnation: the Absolute Spirit is not a changeless form cutting circles in the sky but it has come down to earth and taken human form. That is because the Absolute Spirit cannot think itself all by itself but only in and through human beings thinking the absolute. By the same token, we human beings cannot think the absolute all by ourselves but only with the help of a concrete exemplification, a magnetic individual (Jesus), who is not just an individual man but an intuition of the Absolute. The Absolute thinks itself by our thinking the Absolute. So the Absolute Spirit needs us as much as we need the Absolute Spirit. That is philosophy, German philosophy, of course, and if truth be told, though modesty prevents him from saying it, Hegel's philosophy. For Hegel, what they are singing on Sunday morning in the churches is getting explained during the week in seminars at the Philosophy Department at the University of Berlin, where religious pictures and stories are laid out explicitly in concepts, not in songs and without the bells and smells. Philosophy makes conceptually explicit both what is imaginatively pictured or represented (*vorgestellt*) in religion, and what is sensuously embodied in art works in a darker, more evocative form. Religion has a sensuous side, which summons up a fully embodied sense of being in the Spirit, and a conceptual side (theology). Theopoetics is superseded by theology; religion is superseded by philosophy. In philosophy we finally get the code to read the symbols, the legendum needed to read off the legends of religion, and finally to translate religious representations into the real presence of metaphysical reality.

That is the sort of claim that threw Kierkegaard into spasms. It seems as though God came into the world, Kierkegaard sneered, to arrange a consultation with German metaphysics about the make-up of the divine being. And on this point Tillich sides with Kierkegaard, and both of them are siding with Schelling, who was a critic of Hegel. Tillich too rejected the notion of absolute knowledge. For him, the ground of being was a mystery wrapped in an enigma, and what we say about it will always be symbolic and never absolute. For Tillich, we can never find an unconditional way to speak of the unconditional, never remove the risk and never be free of the need for courage. There is always an irreducible folly, a divine madness about the unconditional, which can never be thought away.

## Quit When You're Ahead

In sum, Hegel's breakthrough, his theopoetics, was to redescribe "Revelation" as a richly imaginative and suggestive figuration of the Spirit—which invites and requires thought—and not as the effect of a revelation from on high, whose boundaries natural reason must observe. The breakthrough was to distinguish between these imaginative figures and *what is going on in* them, which has to be figured out or interpreted, which is what we mean by "hermeneutics." The breakthrough was to see that religion takes shape as a poetics (*Vorstellung*) not a supernatural intervention from on high. The breakthrough was to break the ban on the "revealed contents" of "sacred theology," to invite thinking into the sanctuary, and to ask, what is going on? But door opener though it was, Hegel's coattail got stuck in the door. As deeply indebted to Hegel as I am, and without being churlish, I too agree with Kierkegaard that Hegel is overreaching. I beg to disagree with Hegel about what *is* going on—which I think is the call of the unconditional, not absolute knowledge but the folly of the call, the inbreaking of the "event," that is, the promise/threat of the coming of what we cannot see coming. That, I think, is what is going on in religion and theology, which are the embodiment of our aspirations, not the bodying forth of Absolute Spirit. That entails the folly, the touch of madness, that allows the unconditional to be unconditional.

The task of a theology of the unconditional is twofold. First, it should protect the secrecy of the unconditional, to maintain it in its indefinite mode, to prevent it from being identified with this or that definite being or belief, to keep it safe in its infinitival open-endedness and to refuse to let it be contracted to some definite, finite thing. Secondly, its task is to maintain the unconditional in the weak mode, to protect its weakness from the drift the tides of theology inevitably take toward power, bombast, and authoritarianism. What is going on is the *call* of something unconditional, if there is such a thing, the folly of the call, not "absolute knowledge" of the Absolute Spirit, which is, as Paul said, one of "the pretensions of those who think they know it all" (1 Cor 1:27). I put a kind of non-knowledge just where Hegel put the Absolute Knowledge of Philosophy, a poetics where he put a metaphysics—and so, on this point, I side with Tillich and the searing barbs Kierkegaard launched at Hegel's metaphysics. Metaphysics for me is always driving under the influence, an idea running out of control, and it is bound to crash, thereby posing a danger to itself and others. In its place I put a hermeneutics of experience, where we are exposed to contingency and deep unforeseeability, just where Hegel had put a classical theology still under the spell of Aristotle, where things are ultimately guided by an underlying necessity and Providential guidance, where the unconditional finds a place—philosophy—where it can think itself unconditionally.

In other words, I think Hegel should have quit when he was ahead. He should have stopped at the characterization of religion in terms of the *Vorstellung*. At that point he should have waxed very apophatic and taciturn, refusing to say another word, declining to take another step forward. He should have followed the example of Socrates who said that saying anything more about the Good was for another day, which of course never comes. He should have stopped in his tracks, stayed firm with his theopoetics and not tried to advance to the higher ground of a high theology. Hegel is right to say that religion is a way we have been given to imagine the unconditional—the event—but we weak theologians want no commerce with the next step he took, what he called the Concept, the Absolute Knowledge of the Absolute Spirit, thought thinking itself. That's the DUI. Our only absolute is the absolute unforeseeability of the absolute future, the folly of the call that calls for an unconditional response. Hegel's Absolute Spirit still smacks of the old alliance with the high and mighty discourse of classical metaphysical theology, a point, which, allowing for their differences, I think also applies to Tillich's "ground of being."

So in the place of Hegel's Concept and of Tillich's ground of being I put the inconceivable, unprogrammable event, the coming of what we cannot see coming, the hope in a future we also hope won't be a disaster, and a considerable postmodern incredulity about saying anything more. We defer all absolute knowledge, absolute concepts, absolute spirits; we call for adjourning the meeting of the Department of Absolute Knowledge, *sine die*. In the place of the pretensions of metaphysics we put an unpretentious poetics, the various and irreducibly plural ways we have of giving figure and form to our experience of the unconditional, of giving it narratival and pictorial form, in words and images, striking sayings and dramatic scenes, which is what we mean by a theopoetics of the folly of God. Religion is a song to the unconditional, a way to sing what lays claim to us unconditionally. But as to identifying what the unconditional *is*, if it is, we beg to be excused. This is a hermeneutics where nobody has the key, the code, the legendum. Art, religion and philosophy—and science and ethics and politics and everyday life, everything that is going on in the culture at large—are so many ways to negotiate with the underlying eventiveness of life, of life in time, in life as time, so many ways to inhabit the space between the conditional and the unconditional.

I think of weak theology as a kind of decapitated Hegelianism, Hegel without a Concept, without Absolute Knowledge—all these prestigious German capitals being decapitated, deprived of the upper case. We settle for religion in the lower case, for religion as a *Vorstellung* for which we lack a final interpretation, its testosterone-rich pretensions having been cut down or circum-cut off, left in want of a way to lay out in strong conceptual terms what is calling and getting itself called in religion. The *Vorstellung* goes all the way down, interpretation is endless, resulting in a "radical hermeneutics"[59]—and consequently a radical or weak theology which cannot conceive of any absolute Concept and would in fact prefer not to. Any such Concept would arrest the play not only of religious discourses and practices but of cultural life more generally. Religion and art are ways to give words and form to the unconditional, but the unconditional does not exist; it insists. The unconditional is not an Absolute Spirit or a ground of being but a specter that gives the actual conditioned world no peace. So instead of thinking of religion as the Sabbath of life, a day of rest and refuge, I think of it in terms of a specter that spooks our lives, that makes our hearts restlessness, as a 24/7 alert, an un-Sabbath that gives us no rest and peace. The only real peace is six feet under, *requiescat in pace*, while back here among the living, life is spooked by the specters of the past and of the absolute future.

The spell cast by the gospel is not theological but theopoetic. Weak theology, thus, is theopoetics, the poetics of what is going on in the name (of) "God." By a poetics I mean, in sum, a constellation of metaphors and metonyms, of narratives and songs, of parables and paradoxes, of poems and puzzling sayings, of dazzling images and amazing stories, of rhetorical strategies and apophatic discourses, of strategic reversals and topsy-turvy inversions, all designed to elicit a sense of the event, to disarm the disinterested observers of their distance and to draw them into the fray. A poetics is the discourse proper to the event, because the event is not a form or structure to be delineated, not an essence or a prestigious presence, not one of the powers that be. An event is not a being in time or outside time but a being spooked-by time. It does not yield to an objectivistic discourse and does not have to do with an "object" represented by a "subject," as Tillich said in the text that is the touchstone of this essay. Theopoetics is not a science of presence or of something present, but a poetics of the unconditional. It is not an ontology but a hauntology. Theopoetics concerns something that has no proper name, since names are nominatives, while a poetics gives words to something coming, something infinitival, which means every nominative must be recast in the mode of the to-come, like a democracy-to-come—or a God-to-come. It is not even enough to say that it shifts from the nominal to the verbal, which will only get us as far as process metaphysics, when we set Aristotle's idea of being as substance or stable presence (*ousia*) to the tune of time. A theopoetics has recourse instead to every infinitival, adverbial, and prepositional device at its disposal. As an evocation evoked by a provocation, everything in theopoetics revolves around a call (*vocare*). God does not exist. God calls for existence.

The folly of God is that God is an unconditional call without an army to back it up. The folly of God is that God does not exist; God insists. God's folly is, not clinging to existence, to disappear into an anonymous call, a call which leaves us uncertain about who or what is calling, what is being called for, what is being recalled. Our folly is to answer a call whose provenance is clouded, whose message is obscure, and whose memory is faded. It is the folly to answer an unconditional but uncertain call, where it is up to us to determine what is being called for, which requires us not only to be responsible to the call, but also responsible for it.

## The Kingdom of God

In the scriptures, the folly of God goes under the name of the kingdom of God. The kingdom of God describes what the world would look like when the event that lays claim to us in and under the name of the God holds sway. The kingdom is the world exposed to an event, to the call of the event, to the event of the call, to the folly of what is being called. The spell of the gospel is to have been written under the spell of a call, which calls for the coming of the kingdom, which announces good news for the poor and imprisoned and the year of the Jubilee (Luke 4:18). The gospels are the theopoetics of the call, a felicitous message, good news—not a news report. They are songs sung to the memory and the promise of Yeshua, to the coming again of the one who has already come once, and their penultimate line is "come" (Rev 22:20), songs sung to the kingdom whose coming he proclaimed. It is a simple literary mistake, a basic hermeneutical error, to treat them as attempts to accurately reproduce past history; it is a simple historical mistake, an anachronism, to treat them as biographies in the modern sense. They are not historical accounts but songs of praise. They are not recording past history, but singing about a promise and memory, about a call and a recalling, about an event, and they say "come" to the coming of what they cannot see coming.

Lucky for them. After all, think about it, it did not come, the kingdom—and it did not matter. In fact, nobody thought to write anything down until it began to dawn on them that what is coming will be a long time coming (and we're still waiting). Indeed, what we call "Christianity" depends upon its *not* coming, upon the deferral of the coming—until God knows when! As the groundbreaking Catholic New Testament scholar Abbé de Loisy (1857–1940) once said, the early Christians were waiting for Jesus but what they got

instead was the church! So if Yeshua and Paul were indeed apocalyptic thinkers, they turned out to be mistaken. The church, I like
to say, was Plan B.[60] Yeshua announced the year of the Jubilee for
the Jews and things got even worse. Forty years after Yeshua announced the coming of the kingdom and the year of the Jubilee,
the Temple was destroyed, the Jews were scattered, and the rule
of Rome was firmer than ever. That is the perfectly good reason
that the Jews were less than convinced that Yeshua was the long
awaited Messiah. That means either that the gospels are based
upon a terrible miscalculation and we have to crunch the numbers
one more time—or that Jubilee is not a matter of calculation and
mathematical accuracy. We keep counting and we never get to fifty.
How strange a number is that! How mad a calculation! This Jubi-
larian or Pentecostal fifty is an exceedingly odd number, at least as
odd as the logic of the logos of the cross, or the rule of something
unconditional without an army to enforce its decrees. How much
"evidence" do we need to see that God, the name of God, what is
going on in the name (of) "God" has to do with a poetics and not
the metaphysics of a Supreme Being?

The gospels are no more a set of predictions about the future
than they are a journal of the past; they are a song to the event, a
song celebrating the event. They are a poetics, a theopoetics, of the
event that lays claim to us unconditionally under the name of God.
That explains why the rule of God that they describe is quite unruly.
They depict a topsy-turvy world, a mad, mad world, madder than
the mad hatter's party, in which the first are last and the insiders are
out and sinners are preferred, which is the sort of thing that goes on
under the name of God's "rule." In the kingdom, the strong logic
of a high and mighty theology is displaced by the mad logic of a
theopoetics, a fool's logic (*morologia*), which, as I said at the very
outset, was captured in the logic of the cross in 1 Corinthians 1,
where Paul said the weakness of God is stronger than the strength
of human beings and God's folly stronger than human knowledge.
That is the appeal of the kingdom, which means the folly of the call

which peals in the gospels across the ages, what takes hold of us, however accurate or inaccurate the gospels may be about the facts of the matter and the mathematics. When we call for the kingdom to come, it is because the kingdom first calls to us in them—the kingdom calls for a form of life that is mad about justice and forgiveness, come what may, even unto death.

The only logic in the kingdom is the fool's logic of the cross, and the only power is the powerless power of mercy and forgiveness, and the only rule the unruliness of a topsy-turvy world. The poetics of the kingdom means the paradoxical, parabolic para-logic of the kingdom, the alogic of an ironic kingdom. The folly of this kingdom could only provoke the scorn and the alarm of the people who really ran the kingdom, who ran the real kingdom, the one with an army, the one that exists, while the kingdom-to-come only insists. In comparison with the *Imperium Romanum*, which was the kingdom that was not fooling around, the kingdom with all the real power, the "kingdom of God" and the strength of God's weakness were a joke, although they were a joke that the *Imperium* did not take lightly. But that joke, that irony, the pure folly of that kingdom, was a subversive and dangerous enemy of the powers that be. How could that be?

# 10

# Does the Kingdom of God need God?

Let us assume for the sake of the argument that I have made my case, that I have disabused you of the idea of a high and mighty theology organized around the Supreme Being. If so, it is too soon to celebrate. For that only brings us back to the paradoxical problem posed by this argument. The "kingdom" of God means God's "rule" (*basileia, regnum, imperium*). It refers to what the world would look like when God is our pilot, when God is at the wheel, when the world is subject to the rule of God, and God makes our enemies our footstools. The problem my hypothesis encounters is that there is no mistaking that kingdom talk is high and mighty talk. The kingdom means that at the opportune time (*kairos*) God steps in and takes over the controls and the powers and principalities are scattered, brought to their knees, made to rue the day they were ever so foolish as to take on the Almighty. The coming of the kingdom of God means that the tables are turned and it is the world that is made up of fools and God who is holding all the cards.

Unless it does not.

Unless the "rule" of God is a kind of divine irony, a holding sway that does not hold with violence and power.

Unless the business of the kingdom is conducted according to the logic of the cross.

Unless the kingdom is folly from the point of view of the powers that be in the world, just as Paul says in 1 Corinthians 1.

Unless the kingdom is foolishness in terms of what counts as a kingdom in the world, like a tiny mustard seed growing into a massive tree.

Period, with nothing up our sleeve, a weak force all the way down, with no follow-up chapter in which we take it all back and say that eventually, probably very soon, the enemies of God will be laid low. If not here, then in the hereafter, but eventually we win. The world is all about winning, even and especially under the name of religion, in which the folly of God is a move made in a divine chess game in which the world is completely outsmarted.

My claim is that in speaking of the folly of God, of the name (of) "God," in terms of something unconditional without sovereignty, of a weak force without an army to back it up, of the powerless power of the kiss not of the power of the sword, we are speaking of the kingdom and of God otherwise. We are speaking of another kind of kingdom, a kingdom without a king in the world's sense, in which the world is subject not to the mighty arm of the Almighty King who has come to settle the accounts of the world, but a kingdom subject to the soft sway of something unconditional without power as the world knows power. We are not talking about winning, and we do not use weakness as a strategy in a game in which God finally makes the winning move. In the light of such an ironic rule, of such an unroyal and unruly rule, the image of the Son of Man, the Royal Judge, coming to judge the nations turns out to be another one of those half-blasphemous and mythological figures. It reduces the unconditional to a worldly condition, literalizes it and enters it into a worldly war with the powers and principalities, among which the Son of Man too is to be included, indeed as the final winner.

That means—to come back to our guiding question and to frankly bite the bullet—the folly of God, the folly of the kingdom of God does not need God. In fact, the Supreme Being would ruin everything. But—and everything depends upon what we say next—that is not the end of the kingdom of God. It is the beginning; it does not mean there is nothing to the name (of) "God." This salutary, theological atheism about the Supreme Being does not spell the end of God's kingdom; it dispels the misunderstanding. It does not dispel the gospel's news; it dispels the misunderstanding of the gospel and preserves what is good about the good news. It opens the door to understanding the coming of the kingdom otherwise than in terms of power, and to understanding power otherwise, God's power or anyone else's, to understanding the powerless power of something unconditional but without power as the world knows power.

## Let Your Kingdom Come

To approach this issue let us ask when we pray, "let your kingdom come," are we asking the Supreme Being to intervene in history, to come to our aid and do something down here below in space and time, to make something happen? Are we all then left in suspense waiting for a response, especially as centuries of delay tick away? Does the mystery lie in this, that the kingdom is coming at some future date that remains unknown to all but the Supreme Being? That is the mythological view for which I have tried to make as much trouble as possible. Far from needing theology's Supreme Being to come to our rescue, the coming of the kingdom would actually be impeded by it. Were the Supreme Being to show up, in all his glory, surrounded by all his angels, seated on his throne of glory, the nations arrayed before him (Matt 25:31–32), that would be bad news, the worst. It would prevent the event harbored in the name (of) "God." The rule of God must be otherwise, must be something else. The coming of the kingdom is not an episode scheduled for a future time on the cosmic calendar but the call of an event. The kingdom does not come by way of a dramatic cosmo-theological intervention in history from on high. Fifty is not a number; it is a prayer. God's folly is not just a clever strategy, not a way of sneaking into the enemy's camp at night and taking them by surprise.

The folly of the kingdom is that the kingdom calls, unconditionally but without power, without the power to enforce its call or to reward or threaten its responders. The kingdom is what is called for. Both caller and what is called for, the kingdom is what is getting itself called, in the middle voice, in and under the name of the kingdom. The coming of the kingdom is the call, the promise, of something to-come, while our "come" is the response, the hope, the prayer, the dream of a form of life that lures us on its own and is not enforced from above. The rule of God rises from within the world; it does not descend upon us from on high. The kingdom of God is within us; it is not a powerful force intervening from without. The kingdom runs under the impulse of the events that already pulse through it, rather than being ruled from above by a strong if invisible hand. The kingdom is always to come but it is not a future state of affairs. It is the solicitation here and now of a form of life, one that has already begun and is already here, already solicits us.

The kingdom is found every time the displaced are given shelter and the hungry are fed, every time the poor are comforted, every time the imprisoned are visited. The kingdom comes here and now, insofar as we live here and now under the weak force of its lure, even as it is always still to-come. The "to-come" does not signify a future present but the weak force of a call for something coming. The to-come does not belong to calendar time, but to the crazy clockwork of messianic time. The kingdom is not governed from on high but organized from within by the unconditional call to which it is the response, which constitutes its own integral mode of being-in-the-world, its own particular experience of the unconditional. The rule of God takes place by way of the gentle provocation of a poetics—without a powerful metaphysical theology to back it up; without a Supreme Ruler who dispatches a heavenly host of warrior angels to come to our aid; without an apologetic theology to defend God's rule against its detractors; and without a world-wide system of divinity schools and seminaries to work out its logic and train and commission its emissaries. The rule of God is more unruly, more disarmed, more like outright folly.

The kingdom, *what is going on in the kingdom,* is the weak force of the *event* to which it gives words and deeds. The kingdom comes calling; it comes by calling; it comes with the weak force of the unconditional, if there is such a thing. It is sustained by the insistence of an event that calls unconditionally and that calls for an unconditional response, but without the powers of enforcement. The kingdom peals with the appeal of what calls, of what is being called for, of who is being called upon, not like a trumpet announcing an army's advance. The kingdom takes form in the theopoetics of Yeshua, in the memory and the promise of what he said and did, in his words of unconditional forgiveness, of mercy for the least among us, of freedom for the oppressed, of good news for the poor and the coming year of the jubilee. The kingdom comes by reaching out to the outcasts, sitting down to table with the outsiders, healing the lame and making the blind to see, driving out the demons that possess us all.

Our task has been to follow the logic of the cross, of foolishness and weakening, which means, the logic of letting God be God, no more and no less, where to "let" means that this is not our doing and "be" means what is unconditional without being. Up to now this has meant letting the God of high and mighty theology weaken into a poetics of the event that is harbored in the name (of) "God." Led now by the logic of weakening, we let God weaken into the kingdom of God and we let the kingdom of God weaken into the world, where God has pitched his tent.

The folly of the kingdom of God is the heart of what the phenomenologists call a life-world, a form of life with a practical logic of its own; or what the later Heidegger calls the "worlding of the world," the way the world unfolds as a world of sky and earth, of divinities and mortals; or what the theologians call the "sacrament of the world," where the visible world takes shape under the weak but insistent pressure of the event, of an invisible but unconditional call. The internal logic of the kingdom is the alogic, the folly, of the cross. Its dynamics are the movements of a kenotic abdication of supreme power of a Supreme Being for the powerless power of mercy and compassion. The kingdom does not require a royal agent; it does not require, indeed it does not tolerate, a backup, a foundation, a ground, a cause, a telos, an economic system, all of which would undermine it. The kingdom is the folly of the unconditional, the folly of call that emanates from the face of the stranger, from the bodies of the leper and the needs of the poor and imprisoned. The folly is that it is sustained by that *and nothing more*, because anything more would be too much, a power play that would overwhelm its delicate networks, a way to win, which shrinks the kingdom down to a reward for good behavior. The "rule of God" cannot mean the rule of an omnipotent and sovereign power but an unruly and unroyal rule of a weak force, of a certain sacred impotence and divine folly. The rule of the kingdom does not constitute a hierarchy but a sacred anarchy. After all, the *ikon* of the God in the kingdom of God is an unjustly crucified man who forgave his executioners and whose disciples scattered in the moment of maximum peril. There is no greater folly than that. The kingdom whose coming he announces is not sustained by a show of might but by a certain invisible and weak force.

The evidence on which I rest my case is the folly of the impossible. The coming of the kingdom comes down to the possibility of the impossible. That is decidedly *not* to be confused with literalized feats of water-walking magic performed by a Super Being recorded by eyewitnesses supposedly intent on making an accurate historical report. That's the half-blasphemy, the mythology, the stuff of super-heroes and summer action films. That is the faith of those with little faith, those who do not trust or even want this kingdom unless there is a concealed divine omnipotence behind it to make it all happen and to ensure that, in the end, the just are rewarded and the unjust punished and the friends of God win. The evidence of the impossible is not that it happens but that it does not, that it insists without existence, that it calls without relenting for the coming of what does not come, like the Year of the Jubilee. How foolish is that! We never get to fifty when we start counting up how many years it will be to the Jubilee. How long, O Lord, how long? Forever, for all time, for as long as there is time, for as long as the future is still to come and we cannot see what is coming, for as long as we will be calling "come." The coming kingdom is as a structural matter always a kingdom to-come. May thy kingdom come is a permanent prayer that gives the actual world no rest.

## The Insistence of the Kingdom

The kingdom does not exist; it insists. The coming of the kingdom is not to be confused with a past, present, or future-present state of affairs. It is not an existent, past, present, or future. The kingdom does not exist; it calls. The kingdom is the folly of an unconditional call—a call to live unconditionally, to offer unconditional mercy, hospitality, and forgiveness. It would be mythological and half-blasphemous to literalize it as an existent state of affairs, an episode containable in a geographical place and or datable in calendar time. When it comes to the coming of the kingdom, every land is a holy land, and every day a holy day. Remember the Jewish-Protestant-Deconstructive principle, that no conditioned thing can hold up under the pressure of the unconditional, that the unconditional cannot be confined to such particular conditions. To identify the kingdom with an existent state of affairs, with a future-present existence that will arrive in some future time and place, when God will set up his rule and the powers of the world will scatter, is at least as destructive of it as any attack by cold-hearted atheists. The mythologists of the kingdom erode it from within even as the atheists would attack it from without. It would be the worst mythologization of the kingdom to treat it as a real *imperium* governed by the powers and principalities of a High and Mighty Being, a Supreme Being, asserting supremacy over the powers of the world. That would be to play the game of the powers and principalities. To that the right religious and theological response is a salutary atheism, one with the best interests of the kingdom in mind.

It is not that I do not have a taste for actual existence and the real facts. On the contrary, if you want to stick to the facts, I will be glad to oblige. The facts of the matter surrounding the Jesus of fact, Yeshua from Nazareth, are mostly lost in the fog of history, and they are foggy enough that for a while they even argued about whether he ever existed. The attempt to burn off that fog with the sun of the Christ of Faith is a process of the historical construction of a *Vorstellung* badly in need of further thought. That in turn requires institutions where the right to ask any question is a fact, not a fiction, where it won't cost you your job if you ask too many questions. The road from Nazareth to Nicaea is a construction badly in need of deconstruction.[61] I am happy to stick to the facts, to put my ear to the ground and listen for the echoes of the event that is astir back there in the misty figure of Yeshua, now long dead and not since returned except in the way that all ghosts return, who had something haunting to say about a coming kingdom. If you stick to the facts, you soon see that God is spirit, and the spirit is a specter of an event. To stick to God in spirit and in truth is to respect the spectrality of this truth (John 4:24), and not to conflate the event with a fact of the matter.

The kingdom is sustained not by an army but by an event, and the event does not exist but insists, while the response to the event is the only thing that really does exist. That is what I mean when I say that the existence of God is up to us and that is why God needs the kingdom of God. We are the ones whom God is waiting for, the ones who have been expected to fill up what is lacking in the body of God, to pick up where God leaves off. We are the ones God needs to supply the insistence of God with existence, to make what is being called for in the kingdom of God come true. However much we have to learn from the "death of God" theologies—the theological service they provide is to redirect our attention to the sacrament of the world—a theology of the unconditional means to assist at what Meister Eckhart calls the "birth of God." Like Eckhart, I would retrain the focus of the death of God theologies on life. My claim is that our response, our existence, is the truth of the kingdom of God; it is the way the kingdom comes true, which is the way the kingdom comes, if it comes. The coming of the kingdom is its coming true in us, in our response. The truth of the kingdom of God is such existence as God enjoys, such existence as the event that insists in the name of God enjoys.

As theology becomes theopoetics, theopoetics becomes theopraxis. Theology wanes into theopoetics and theopoetics waxes into theopraxis. The waning of the logos is the waxing of the praxis. That means that the weakness of God requires our strength to make God whole, and the folly of God is to let so much depend upon us. The folly of God requires our courage to take a risk on God. The unconditional demands our strength to respond to what calls upon us under the particular conditions in which we find ourselves. The kingdom calls, the kingdom is what is called for, the kingdom is always already being recalled—the rest is up to us. Nothing is guaranteed. Nothing says that the worst will not happen. No invisible hand ensures a good outcome. No Providence guides it like a ship to a safe harbor. Nothing says that the good will triumph and the evil will repent their ways or be punished. The event means the coming of what we cannot see coming and nothing says that it will all end well. To pray for the coming of the kingdom is an exercise of hope.

## Precious, Perfect Folly

The kingdom is sustained best, indeed it can only be sustained at all, when it abides by the searing, searching, and simple account of the unconditional in Matthew:

> Lord, when was it that we saw you hungry and gave you food, or thirsty and gave you something to drink? And when was it that we saw you a stranger and welcomed you, or naked and

gave you clothing? And when was it that we saw you sick or in prison and visited you? (25:37–39)

The text describes the works of mercy with merciless simplicity—when we feed the hungry and quench their thirst, when we clothe the naked, welcome the stranger, visit the imprisoned, and care for the sick. What interests me about this text is that all these works are carried out in the weak mode, or in the mode of folly—by which I mean in the absence of any deeper cause or purpose to be attained, of any Categorical Imperative or Divine Command, of any promises or threats. If there are rewards at stake here they are an absolute secret. These works are undertaken unconditionally. Love does not exist; love calls. Love is a weak force, not one of the powers and principalities that threaten reprisal if it is not heeded and promises a reward if it is. The works of love are performed "without why," as the mystics say, on the grounds that love is always "without why."[62] If love is love it does not have anything up its sleeve. If you ask two people why they love, what they hope to get out of this love affair, they would be nonplussed. Any answer as they might muster would be circular; they would just end up saying because love is love. The works of mercy, which are works of love of the other, friend or foe (*hostis*), are performed without anything else in view, without knowledge of or motivation by some deeper reason to do them. They represent a gift in the truest sense, undertaken unconditionally, done without the expectation of a reward or the fear of punishment. They are a precious, perfect folly.

Recall our earlier discussion (chapter 3) of the string quartet on the Titanic that continued to play its beautiful music in the face of an impending disaster. The music was not going to upright the ship; their playing was undertaken unconditionally, without the expectation of a reward. This example helps us widen the amplitude of the folly of the kingdom of God so that it is not confused with or confined to religion in the narrow sense. All such deeds are, in Paul's terms, folly. For Aristotle they are *kalon*, beautiful, noble.

In Derrida's terms, they are a gift, not an economic exchange. In Deleuze's terms, they are the way we make ourselves worthy of the events that happen to us. In Lyotard's terms, they are carried out without the least knowledge of any Big Story in which they are playing their appointed part.

What Big Story? The half-blasphemous and mythological one that turns love into one of the powers and principalities, a Strong Force in the world that makes our enemies our footstool. Like the one about the coming of the "Son of Man." Before it was reworked by these Greek-speaking gentile followers of Jesus, this expression simply meant a simple man of flesh and bones, a mortal man, one of the nothings and nobodies of the world to whom Paul was writing at Corinth (1 Cor 1:25). But by the time of Matthew 25 the Son of Man is one of the mythological forces, one of the powers that be, one of the powers and principalities, a High and Mighty Being coming to judge the nations, to separate out the sheep from the goats.[63] When this royal judge—this is what has become of defeated, crucified Yeshua—arrives, he will tell the faithful that a great treasure awaits them, that they have been granted entry to the kingdom as reward (*merces*) for having performed these works of mercy. How so? the merciful will rightly ask, having had no such thing on their mind. These people were hungry, thirsty, naked, sick, and imprisoned, and that was the beginning and the end of it. That was all that mattered. They intended nothing else. The claim made upon them by those in need speaks for itself. The call calls, unconditionally, but without force. They could have walked away, but instead they responded. Why? It may seem a little mad, but they chose to love, rather than not. If it was a little mad, it was with the madness of the kingdom. It has no further "reason" than that. If love has a reason, if it has been entirely relieved of folly, if it all makes good sense, you can be sure what is going on is something other than love.

What need is there, what neediness drives us to say anything *more*? What need is there to make this stronger, to amplify it, to supply it with heft and punch and power? Why add anything else?

What else is there to add? But religion cannot resist a chance to make a profit. Everything depends upon how we read the famous reply made by the royal judge: "Just as you did it to one of the least of these who are members of my family, you did it to me" (Matt 25:40). Taken in its weak mode, left in the mode of folly, submitted to the condition of the unconditional, that is the beginning, the middle, and the end. There is nothing else to say. The figure of Jesus *is* a figure of solidarity with those who have been beaten down by the powers of this world, with the least among us. Jesus is the *ikon* of the nothings and nobodies of the world, who bear the mark of God, of the weakness God, on brows bloodied and beaten but unbowed. These afflicted people *are* the body of God and those who responded to their afflictions were filling up what is lacking in the body of God. That is all! The mark of a good storyteller is to know when the story is over and not to keep on talking. The merciful are responding to the call that is called unconditionally in and from these afflicted bodies, making the kingdom of God happen, making it come to pass in the bodies of the hungry, naked, and imprisoned, supplying the insistence of the call with real existence in a brutal world. See how they love one another. How? Without why. Thus does the kingdom come. Period. The end.

But the eyes of the teller of this story grow large with the prospect of a profitable economy. He has bigger ideas than that and a taller tale to tell. For the author of Matthew 25 there is serious income to be had here, not the incoming of the event, the madness of the kingdom, which loves without why, but *real* income, the income that is coming from the *ens realissimum*, real celestial income. Of this these simple-minded merciful ones are evidently ignorant but the author will disabuse them of their ignorance, like someone showing up at our door to give us the good news that we have inherited a fortune from a relative we didn't know existed. Don't be foolish, the author of the story says, there is profit to be made here. The innocence of these works of mercy is pure gold! It is worth a fortune in eternal rewards. These works are then inserted within a great cosmic story, made a party to a massive cosmic economy, in which these merciful deeds acquire serious celestial value. For the teller of this Big Story about the judgment of the nations, the kingdom is not to be found *in* these deeds but it is bestowed as a reward *for* these deeds. The kingdom comes as a celestial reward for feeding the hungry. But there is more. Every economy includes both credits and debits. When it comes to the coins of the celestial realm there is always another side of the coin: What about those who ignored the afflicted? The story has a place for them too, an accursed place, for they are "accursed" and condemned to "eternal fire" (Matt 25:41). Here they are to be subjected to unimaginable suffering, from which the only relief would be death and so, of course, this suffering is worse than death, intensified as it is by the impossibility of death. Instead of Yeshua, a master of forgiveness, the Royal Judge is a master of retaliation, visiting an infinite fury on the offender.

By now the account of the works of mercy, originally performed without any knowledge of any promised rewards or punishment, has been distorted into a great economic schema, a "half-blasphemous and mythological" account of royal rewards for the merciful and a merciless punishment for those who did not practice the works of mercy. The Son of Man enters into combat with the powers and principalities, thereby becoming one of them, even more fierce and furious than are they, proving himself their better by overpowering them! The wine of the works of mercy is converted into the water of mercenaries. The folly of the kingdom of God turns out to be the good sense of winning an eternal reward. For *after hearing this story*, their original innocence is destroyed. *After hearing this story*, the word will go out among the merciful: *do not be a fool*; feed every hungry one you see—the rewards are unimaginable, the punishments unendurable! The Son of Man comes seated on a throne of celestial economics, a chief accountant of sheep and goats, a keeper of credits and debits, a cashier of rewards and cruelty. All this out of love!—can you believe it? Nietzsche quips.[64] No wonder Nietzsche thought that the logic of the cross was a thin disguise for the logic of resentment. The kingdom of God is entered into a transaction where it is offered as a reward. So conceived, the kingdom of God ends up corrupting the works of love, selling these acts of unconditional mercy for thirty pieces of celestial silver.

In a weak theology, on the other hand, just as God weakens into the kingdom of God, the kingdom of God weakens into the works of mercy. In a theology of the unconditional, the works of mercy do not earn the *reward* of the kingdom of God; the works of mercy *are* the kingdom of God. That confusion of the two is the deep corruption—the mythology, the half-blasphemy—of the kingdom introduced by the author of Matthew 25. The kingdom is the kingdom of the unconditional, of the first responders on the scene to an unconditional call, the call which calls for a cup of cold water for the stranger, for care for the sick, which calls this call unconditionally. With the advent of Neoplatonism, this celestial economy and its pre-Copernican cosmology become part of a dualistic metaphysics of time and eternity, of body and soul, this life and some other, here and hereafter. The eternal is the reward for time, eternal life the return on coping with the trials of temporal life. The good news is that sweaty, dirty, and needy bodies, which are exposed to hunger, cold, and nakedness, which grow old and sick and die, may now be exchanged for incorruptible bodies. Weakness is traded in for strength; every sorrow is paid back with eternal joy; every tear is counted and invested in eternal funds; this wretched corruptible body can be upgraded into a maintenance-free incorruptible one that comes equipped with an (eternal) lifetime guarantee. Life is traded in for life-after-death—sometimes even gladly; wanting to be a martyr is an ancient problem—counting on the terms of the deal that is on the table: that death is the doorway to eternal life. Religion finds this economy irresistible. It cannot resist this line, this lure of power and of final triumph—of making our enemies our footstool, the lure of the final fist-pump of *winning*. "Where, O death, is your victory?" (1 Cor 15:55). That is the religion that leaves Lacan in despair: we fall for it over and over again; it always *wins*.

Win it might, but it loses everything worth having; it makes a mockery, a half-blasphemous and mythological mockery, of the event that is called for and recalled in the gospels. Or better, the event makes a mockery of it! God, the name of God, the event that is harbored in the name (of) "God," is the name of a call to lead an unconditional life, a life that responds to an unconditional call, without hypostasizing the call and treating it as one of the powers and principalities, without subjecting it to the condition of a Supreme Being, and without, in particular, inscribing it in conditions as cynical as the story of the judgment of the nations in Matthew 25. There the children of the light prove to be smarter than the children of the world. Is it not a good deal smarter to invest in celestial goods that are moth-proof and do not rust as opposed to buying long term pain for short term gains that will rust out in no time? The author of Matthew 25 makes nonsense of the folly of God.

## Enough Said

That is why I am arguing that the interest of theology, its best interests, do not lie in a Supreme Being. What has gone so badly wrong in passages like Matthew 25? The distortion of the event by the mythological and half-blasphemous concept of the Supreme Being, the super-agent capable of cutting eternal deals, of dishing out eternal rewards to his (no apologies for the gendered talk) friends and dealing eternal suffering to his enemies; the intimidating bully who responds to those who question his questionable ways by shouting in their ear, where were you when I fashioned the heavens and the earth? (A question on which contemporary physics has since turned the tables, so that we are now wondering more and more, where were *you*!) Once we literalize the unconditional into a character in a story, we have to put up with his character flaws. Add to this mythologizing personification the irresistible temptation to confuse one's own person with the Super-Person, whose ear we are sure we have, and to authorize ourselves to speak on his behalf, and you have the perfect storm. The distortion of a theology of the unconditional by puffing it up into a high and mighty theology of a Super-Being is in no one's true interests, God or human or beast. The kingdom runs on the steam of the unconditional: the folly of gifts given unconditionally, of hospitality offered without screening in advance the stranger who knocks on my door; the folly of forgiving without demanding in advance that the offender meet the conditions that merit forgiveness. If you have to merit forgiveness, there is nothing giving about the forgiving; it's just a deal, the way a bank "forgives" a debt only if you pay off every last cent you owe it. And when banks do distribute "gifts," they are only trying to sell you something!

The unconditionality of the call is a function of its purity, and the purity of the call is a function of keeping the call pure of existence, maintaining it in its inexistence. It is pure not with the purity of Christian Neoplatonic immaterialism but with the purity of unconditional insistence, with a hermeneutic purity, the purity proper to a call that insists, but does not exist, the purity of pure folly. Recall the Protestant/Jewish/Deconstructive principle, and its double injunction:

1. Do not confuse the conditional (deconstructible) with the unconditional (undeconstructible). Do not confuse the unconditional call with a super-existent entity who calls. The essence of a mythological operation is to posit some power out there doing all this and keeping order from on high. Preserve the call in its inexistent unconditionality.

2. Remember that in all this we play the role of the *justus et peccator,* both sinners and justified by faith. We are not doing anything other than letting God be God. We are not big, high-powered autonomous subjects with the power to weaken God. We are accused, placed in the accusative, called upon to respond. Autonomous agents are tricks of light created in the

Enlightenment, even as the Supreme Being is a trick of the light of Revelation.

The reason the disciples did not see their Lord is because the name of the Lord is not the name of a visible existing being, but of an invisible, inexistent, and unconditional call that rises up from the bodies of the hungry, thirsty, and imprisoned. Blessed are those who believe and who do not see. The Messiah is not the name of a Superagent coming to reward and punish. We are the messianic people; *we* are the ones that the dead have been waiting for. *We* are the ones that God has been waiting for. *We* are the ones who are on the spot, called upon, called out, called to act.

The kingdom of God does not need God. Not if the name of God is the name of a Supreme Being, for then everything about the kingdom of God is distorted. We must let God, the name (of) "God," weaken into the name of an event, of an unconditional call, into the folly of a call to lead an unconditional life. It is God, the name of the still soft voice of an insistent call, that has need of the kingdom, of those who will make the kingdom come true in word and deed. The kingdom of God is an auto-organizing complex, taking place in the middle voice, in and under the web of conditions that Derrida nicknamed *différance*. The kingdom of God is something that circulates within these quasi-systems of forces, under its own inner impulses, pulsing with the pulse of the event, not being ruled from on high. We in turn must make ourselves worthy of the event that happens to us in and under this name. The kingdom runs without a back-up Economy, without a First Cause, without an Ultimate Enforcer of its Economy, without a back-up metaphysics to frame it all within a Big Cosmic Story. The call calls ever so softly, without surround-sound cosmic amplification. It is its own form of life, its own mode of being-in-the-world. The call is drowned out by the loud logic of theologic and the apologies of apologetics, by the bombast and intimidation of divine command acoustics, by stockbrokers of eternity hustling us with offers of living forever.

The call calls only by means of the still and quiet promptings of a theopoetics.

The call calls. It calls from the bodies of the hungry and naked and imprisoned, and recalls the body of the crucified one, setting off the sparks of a response, short flickers of light that disappear into the dark.

The call calls. The call calls for a response, which may or may not transpire. God insists, while existence is up to us. The call is not a Mighty Spirit, but a soft aspiration, the soft sighs of a perhaps. The call is not a mighty being but a might-be. The call is not the ground of being, or the being of beings, but a may-being. What is coming is the possibility of the impossible, which we desire with a desire beyond desire, with all the madness of the kingdom, where the only rule is the unruly rule of unconditional gifts.

The call calls. Unconditionally. We love because we love, with all the felicitous folly of love. What else is there to say? The genuine apophaticism is to know when to shut up, to know when silence is praise (*silentia tibi laus*).

"Lord, when was it that we saw you hungry and gave you food, or thirsty and gave you something to drink? And when was it that we saw you a stranger and welcomed you, or naked and gave you clothing? And when was it that we saw you sick or in prison and visited you?" (Matt 25:37–39).

Good question. Enough said.

# Notes

1. Scholars Version translation in *The Authentic Letters of Paul: A New Reading of Paul's Rhetoric and Meaning*.

2. I have worked out these matters in a more detailed and documented way and for an academic audience in Caputo, *The Weakness of God* and *The Insistence of God*, to which the present essay is intended as both an amplification and an introduction for a wider audience. The titles of the three books are exactly symmetric and makes for a kind of postmodern treatise on the divine names which I did not set out to write but which managed to write itself into the script. I will supply references to the academic literature in the endnotes for those who are interested. See also John D. Caputo, "The Weakness of God," in *The Wisdom and Foolishness of God: First Corinthians 1–2 in Theological Exploration*.

3. This is the enduring point made by Bultmann; see his *Jesus Christ and Mythology*.

4. Tillich, *Theology of Culture*, 25.

5. Dawkins, *The God Delusion*; Dennett, *Breaking the Spell*; Harris, *The End of Faith*; Hitchens, *God is Not Great*.

6. Colledge and McGinn, *Meister Eckhart*, 200.

7. Even Tillich speaks of the "God above God," but by "above" he means the depth dimension of God! See Tillich, *The Courage to Be*, 186–90.

8. Tillich, *The Protestant Era*, 32n1.

9. Tillich, *The Courage to Be*, 185.

10. There are libraries in Catholic universities full of this literature, but the classic text is probably Gilson, *The Christian Philosophy of St. Thomas Aquinas*. Modesty prevents me referring to my *Heidegger and Aquinas*, 122–45, where I spent some time detailing this point.

11. The so-called "ontological argument" is introduced thus: "Therefore, Lord, you who grant understanding to faith, grant that ... I may understand that you exist as we believe you exist. ..." Anselm, *Monologion and Proslogion*, chap. 2, p. 99.

12. See for example Marion, "Is the Ontological Argument Ontological?"

13. The argument of Caputo, *What Would Jesus Deconstruct?* is that postmodern theory is good news for the church.

14. Derrida, "Circumfession: Fifty-nine Periods and Periphrases," 155.

129

15. Husserl founded the school of phenomenology, which provides a sensitive rendering of concrete lived experience, as opposed to an abstract theory or causal explanation of it. This was the stock in trade of Heidegger and many major Continentalist philosophers in the Twentieth Century.

16. I tried to provide a readable commentary on Derrida's view on *différance* and other basic matters in *Deconstruction in a Nutshell*. This contains a roundtable with Derrida in which he is clear as a bell, accompanied by my commentary on this roundtable.

17. Malabou, *The Future of Hegel*.

18. Derrida, *Of Grammatology*, 6–10.

19. Derrida, "Faith and Knowledge."

20. See Caputo, "Proclaiming the Year of the Jubilee." This piece is directed to a wider public, not a strictly academic audience.

21. Derrida, *Specters of Marx*, 174. See Caputo, *The Prayers and Tears of Jacques Derrida*, 118–51 for a closer commentary.

22. Augustine, *Confessions*, Book One, chap. 1, p. 3.

23. That is the thesis of Caputo, *The Insistence of God*; see pp. 24–38.

24. For help here I recommend the superb account in Pieper, *The Four Cardinal Virtues*.

25. In *The Gift of Death*, p. 65, Derrida quotes with approval Kierkegaard's saying that the moment of decision, when we have to get off the fence, is a moment of madness.

26. See Caputo, "The Invention of Revelation."

27. Derrida, "Circumfession: Fifty-nine Periods and Periphrases." See my commentary on this difficult text in Caputo, *The Prayers and Tears of Jacques Derrida*, 281–307.

28. Heidegger, "Phenomenology and Theology."

29. Peter Brown, "Introduction," Augustine, *Confessions*, p. xiii. See Caputo, *The Prayers and Tears of Jacques Derrida*, 295 for a commentary.

30. Chrétien, "The Wounded Word."

31. Augustine, *Confessions*, Book Ten, chaps. 6–7, pp. 176–78.

32. Lacan, *The Triumph of Religion Preceded by Discourse to Catholics*, 64.

33. I cite here an expression used by Gilles Deleuze (1925–95), one of the luminary 68ers, found in his *The Logic of Sense*, 149.

34. Žižek, a Slovenian who writes in English, is arguably the most popular philosopher in the western world and certainly its most colorful; he is a leading theorist of culture, who draws upon the work of Hegel and Lacan to analyze, well, just about anything.

35. I make a case for hope in *Hoping Against Hope: Confessions of a Postmodern Pilgrim* (Minneapolis: Fortress Press, 2015).

36. For a nice statement of Vattimo's theological standpoint, see his *After Christianity*.

37. Derrida, *Rogues: Two Essays on Reason*, xiv.

38. Derrida, "The University without Conditions."

39. Derrida, "Force of Law," in Anidjar, *Acts of Religion*; see in particular pp. 242–45. The version available in Cornell, *Deconstruction and the Possibility of Justice*, is earlier.

40. Benjamin, "On the Concept of History," 390. This little essay is very famous and influential and well repays study.

41. That is a big part of the argument of *The Authentic Letters of Paul*.

42. Martin, *The Corinthian Body*, 62.

43. Derrida, *Cosmopolitanism and Forgiveness*. The occasion of the text was a debate in France about whether there should be a statute of limitations on crimes against humanity.

44. In addition to *Cosmopolitanism and Forgiveness*, see "Hostipitality," in Anidjar, *Acts of Religion*.

45. *Kierkegaard's Writings*, vol. VI, 32.

46. Levinas, *Otherwise than Being or Beyond Essence*. This book is exceptionally challenging. A good place to begin reading Levinas is *Totality and Infinity*.

47. There would be a way to radicalize Tillich by re-reading Tillich in terms of Schelling, who describes God as both ground and abyss, hence as having a dark side that God manages to keep in check, whereas we do not. A longer treatment of Tillich would have to examine the extent to which Tillich has incorporated this side of Schelling, who was Tillich's own point of departure. See *Retrieving the Radical Tillich*, ed. Russell Re Manning.

48. This is the argument of Marion, *God Without Being*. Marion is, I think, the leading Catholic philosopher of the day.

49. Derrida shows the several voices of mystical theology in "How to Avoid Speaking: Denials."

50. Lyotard, *The Postmodern Condition*, xxiii–xxiv.

51. Caputo, *The Insistence of God*, 3–23, 259–63.

52. Derrida elaborates this trope throughout *Politics of Friendship*; see pp. 26–48.

53. Heidegger, *Being and Time*, 317–25 (§§56–57).

54. Heidegger, *Being and Time*, 320–21.

55. Heidegger, *Being and Time*, 319.

56. Aristotle, *Metaphysics*, Book XII.

57. See my account of truth, and in particular of Hegel's concept of truth, in Caputo, *Truth*, chap. 5.

58. My account of Hegel is drawn from *Hegel's Lectures on the Philosophy of Religion*. On the concept of *Vorstellung* (representation), see pp. 432–70.

59. A phrase I sometimes use to describe my project in the largest terms ever since I published *Radical Hermeneutics*.

60. Caputo, *What Would Jesus Deconstruct?*, 31–35.

61. See the masterful overview of the genesis of Christianity in Vermes, *Christian Beginnings*.

62. This phrase, first used by the Rhineland mystics, has acquired currency in contemporary thought by way of a verse from Angelus Silesius, *The Cherubinic Wanderer*, 54, which was commented upon by Heidegger, *The Principle of Reason*, 32–40. It is found in Meister Eckhart in *The Complete Mystical Works of Meister Eckhart*, 110. Eckhart himself likely found it in Porete, *The Mirror of Simple Souls*. The relationship between Heidegger and Eckhart was the subject of my first scholarly project: *The Mystical Element in Heidegger's Thought*.

63. Crossan, *Jesus: A Revolutionary Biography*, 49–53.

64. Nietzsche, *The Genealogy of Morals and Ecce Homo*, second essay, chap. xxi, p. 92. Derrida comments on this text at the end of *The Gift of Death*, 114–15.

# Bibliography

Anidjar, Gil, ed. *Jacques Derrida: Acts of Religion.* New York and London: Routledge, 2002.

Anselm. *Monologion and Proslogion.* Trans. Thomas Williams. Indianapolis: Hackett Publishing Co., 1995.

Augustine, *Confessions.* Trans. F. J. Sheed, Introduction Peter Brown. Indianapolis: Hackett Publishing Company, Inc., 1970.

Benjamin, Walter. "On the Concept of History." Pp. 389–400 in *Walter Benjamin: Selected Writings,* Vol. 4, *1938–40.* Ed. Michael Jennings. Cambridge, MA: Belknap Press of Harvard University Press, 2003.

Bultmann, Rudolf. *Jesus Christ and Mythology.* New York: Charles Scribner's Sons, 1958.

Caputo, John D. and Jacques Derrida, *Deconstruction in a Nutshell: A Conversation with Jacques Derrida.* Edited with commentary. New York: Fordham University Press, 1997.

———. *Heidegger and Aquinas: An Essay on Overcoming Metaphysics.* New York: Fordham University Press, 1982.

———. *Hoping Against Hope: Confessions of a Postmodern Pilgrim.* Minneapolis: Fortress Press, 2015.

———. *The Insistence of God: A Theology of Perhaps.* Bloomington: Indiana University Press, 2013.

———. "The Invention of Revelation: A Hybrid Hegelian Approach with a Dash of Deconstruction." Pp. 73–92 in *Revelation: Claremont Studies in the Philosophy of Religion, Conference 2012.* Eds. I. U. Dalferth and M. Ch. Rodgers. Tübingen: Mohr Siebeck, 2014.

———. *The Mystical Element in Heidegger's Thought.* Athens: Ohio University Press, 1978. (Revised, paperback edition with a new Introduction. New York: Fordham University Press, 1986.)

———. *The Prayers and Tears of Jacques Derrida: Religion without Religion.* Bloomington: Indiana University Press, 1997.

———. "Proclaiming the Year of the Jubilee: Thoughts on a Spectral Life." Pp. 10–47 in *It Spooks: Living in Response to an Unheard Call.* Ed. Erin Schendzielos. Rapid City, SD: Shelter 50 Publishing Collective, 2015.

———. *Radical Hermeneutics: Repetition, Deconstruction, and the Hermeneutic Project.* Bloomington: Indiana University Press, 1987.

———. *Truth.* London: Penguin Books, 2013.

———. *What Would Jesus Deconstruct? The Good News of Postmodernity for the Church*. Grand Rapids, MI: Baker Publishing Group, 2007.

———. *The Weakness of God: A Theology of the Event*. Bloomington: Indiana University Press, 2006.

Chalamet, Christophe and Hans-Christoph Askani, eds. *The Wisdom and Foolishness of God: First Corinthians 1–2 in Theological Exploration*. Minneapolis: Fortress Press, 2015.

Chrétien, Jean-Louis. "The Wounded Word: Phenomenology of Prayer." Pp. 121–26 in *Phenomenology and the "theological turn."* Eds. Dominic Janicaud, et al. Trans. B. G. Prusak, J. L. Kosky and T. A. Carlson. New York: Fordham University Press, 2000.

Colledge, Edmund, and Bernard McGinn, trans. *Meister Eckhart: The Essential Sermons, Commentaries, Treatises and Defense*. New York: Paulist Press, 1981.

Crossan, John Dominic. *Jesus: A Revolutionary Biography*. San Francisco: HarperSanFrancisco, 1994.

Dawkins, Richard. *The God Delusion*. Boston: Houghton Mifflin, 2006.

Deleuze, Gilles. *The Logic of Sense*. Trans. Mark Lester with Charles Stivale. Ed. Constantin V. Boundas. New York: Columbia University Press, 1969.

Dennett, Daniel. *Breaking the Spell: Religion As a Natural Phenomenon*. New York: Penguin, 2006.

Derrida, Jacques. "Circumfession: Fifty-nine Periods and Periphrases." Pp. 1–322, in Geoffrey Bennington and Jacques Derrida, *Jacques Derrida*. Chicago: University of Chicago Press, 1993.

———. *Cosmopolitanism and Forgiveness*. Trans. Mark Dooley and Michael Hughes. London and New York: Routledge, 1997.

———. *The Gift of Death*. Trans. David Wills. Chicago: University of Chicago Press, 1995.

———. "Faith and Knowledge: The Two Sources of 'Religion' at the Limits of Reason Alone." Trans. Samuel Weber. Pp. 40–101 in Anidjar, *Acts of Religion*. Also available as pp. 1–78 in *Religion*. Eds. Jacques Derrida and Gianni Vattimo. Stanford: Stanford University Press, 1998.

———. "Force of Law: The 'Mystical Foundation of Authority.'" Trans. Mary Quantaince. Pp. 228–98 in Anidjar, *Acts of Religion*. Also available as pp. 3–69 in *Deconstruction and the Possibility of Justice*. Ed. Drucilla Cornell et al. New York: Routledge, 1992.

———. "Hostipitality." Pp. 356–420 in Anidjar, *Acts of Religion*.

———. "How to Avoid Speaking: Denials." Pp. 73–142 in *Derrida and Negative Theology*. Eds. Howard Coward and Toby Foshay. Albany: SUNY Press, 1992.

———. *Of Grammatology*. Corrected ed. Trans. Gayatri Spivak. Baltimore: Johns Hopkins University Press, 1997.

———. *Politics of Friendship.* Trans. George Collins. London & New York: Verso, 1997.

———. *Rogues: Two Essays on Reason.* Trans. Pascale-Anne Brault and Michael Naas. Stanford: Stanford University Press, 2005.

———. *Specters of Marx: The State of the Debt, the Work of Mourning, and the New International.* Trans. Peggy Kamuf. New York: Routledge, 1994.

———. "The University without Condition." Pp. 202–37 in *Without Alibi.* Ed. and trans. Peggy Kamuf. Stanford: Stanford University Press, 2002.

Dewey, Arthur J., et al., eds. *The Authentic Letters of Paul: A New Reading of Paul's Rhetoric and Meaning.* The Scholars Version. Salem, OR: Polebridge Press, 2010.

Gilson, Etienne. *The Christian Philosophy of St. Thomas Aquinas.* Notre Dame, IN: University of Notre Dame Press, 1994.

Harris, Sam. *The End of Faith: Religion, Terror, and the Future of Reason.* New York: Norton, 2004.

Hegel, Georg Wilhelm Friedrich. *Hegel's Lectures on the Philosophy of Religion,* One Volume Edition: *The Lectures of 1827.* Ed. Peter Hodgson. Berkeley: University of California Press, 1988.

Heidegger, Martin. *Being and Time.* Trans. John Macquarrie and Edward Robinson. New York: Harper & Row, 1962.

———. "Phenomenology and Theology." Pp. 63–81 in *Pathmarks.* Ed. W. McNeill. Cambridge: Cambridge University Press, 1998.

———. *The Principle of Reason.* Trans. Reginald Lilly. Bloomington: Indiana University Press, 1991.

Hitchens, Christopher. *God is Not Great: How Religion Poisons Everything.* New York: Twelve, 2007.

Kierkegaard, Søren. *Kierkegaard's Writings, VI, Fear and Trembling and Repetition.* Trans. and ed. Howard and Edna Hong. Princeton: Princeton University Press, 1983.

Lacan, Jacques. *The Triumph of Religion Preceded by Discourse to Catholics.* Trans. Bruce Fink. Cambridge: Polity Press, 2013.

Levinas, Emmanuel. *Otherwise Than Being or Beyond Essence.* Trans. Alphonso Lingis. The Hague: Nijhoff, 1981.

———. *Totality and Infinity: Essay on Exteriority.* Trans. Alphonso Lingis. Pittsburgh: Duquesne University Press, 1969.

Lyotard, Jean-François. *The Postmodern Condition: A Report on Knowledge.* Trans. Geoff Bennington and Brian Massumi. Minneapolis: University of Minnesota Press, 1984.

Malabou, Catherine. *The Future of Hegel: Plasticity, Temporality and Dialectic.* Trans. Lisabeth During. New York: Routledge, 2005.

Manning, Russell Re, ed. *Retrieving the Radical Tillich: His Legacy and Contemporary Significance.* New York: Palgrave Macmillan, 2015.

Marion, Jean-Luc. *God without Being*. Trans. Thomas Carlson. Chicago: University of Chicago Press, 1991.

———. "Is the Ontological Argument Ontological?" *Journal of the History of Philosophy* 30,2 (1992) 201–18.

Martin, Dale B. *The Corinthian Body*. New Haven: Yale University Press, 1995.

Meister Eckhart. *The Complete Mystical Works of Meister Eckhart*. Trans. and ed. Maurice O'C. Walshe. New York: Crossroad, 2009.

Nietzsche, Friedrich. *The Genealogy of Morals and Ecce Homo*. Trans. W. Kaufmann and F. J. Hollingdale. New York: Random House, Vintage Books, 1969.

Pieper, Josef. *The Four Cardinal Virtues*. Notre Dame, IN: University of Notre Dame Press, 1966.

Porete, Marguerite. *The Mirror of Simple Souls*. Trans. Ellen L. Babinsky. New York: Paulist Press, 1993.

Silesius, Angelus. *The Cherubinic Wanderer*. Trans. Maria Shrady. New York: Paulist Press, 1986.

Tillich, Paul. *The Courage to Be*. New Haven: Yale University Press, 1952.

———. *The Protestant Era*. Abridged ed. Chicago: University of Chicago Press, 1957.

———. *Theology of Culture*. Oxford: Oxford University Press, 1959.

Vattimo, Gianni. *After Christianity*. Trans. Luca D'Isanto. New York: Columbia University Press, 2002.

Vermes, Geza. *Christian Beginnings: From Nazareth to Nicaea*. New Haven: Yale University Press, 2013.

# Index

Anselm, 20–21
apophatic, 22, 34, 69–70, 85, 92, 104,
    106, 128
    see "mysticism"
Aquinas, Thomas, 15–16, 94
Aristotle, 23, 24, 36, 54, 94, 96, 101,
    103, 106, 120
atheism
    Derrida and, 23, 43–44
    conventional forms of, 11, 73–74
    theological form of , 2, 9–14, 66–
        67, 74–77, 96, 112–13, 118
    see "Tillich, atheism of"
Augustine, 13, 14, 34, 70, 78, 84
    Derrida and, 43–46
Balthasar, Hans Urs von, 20
Barth, Karl, 20, 39
Benjamin, Walter, 57–58
call, the, 83–92
    folly of, 87–92, 106–7, 109, 116
    of justice, 56–58
    of the kingdom of God, 107–9,
        113–15, 117–19
    of the unconditional, 28–30, 34, 39,
        49–50, 63, 80, 88–92, 103–4, 115,
        119, 121–22, 124–28
Chrétien, Jean-Louis, 45
Courage, moral vs. courage to be,
    41–43, 53, 102, 119
deconstruction, 21–24, 67, 68, 118
    auto-deconstruction, 26
    the deconstructible and, 24–28
    event in, 24–28, 45, 49–50, 52, 63,
        68, 78–81, 85–86, 90, 94–96, 100,
        103–6, 107, 108, 113–15, 118–19,
        122, 125, 127
    hauntology and, 30, 33–34, 35, 36,
        49–50, 57–58, 78, 106, 118
    the impossible and, 38–40, 45
    the Jewish Principle and, 31–34
    post-structuralism and, 26–27

religion and, 35–36, 39, 43, 49–50
    the undeconstructible and, 28–30, 39
Deleuze, Gilles, 121
    on the event, 49
democracy, see "Derrida"
Derrida, Jacques, 22
    Augustine and, 43–46
    democracy and, 33, 38, 84–85, 106
    différance and, 24, 83–84, 86, 127
    forgiveness and, 62
    the gift and, 38, 63, 120–21, 126,
        128
    hospitality and, 62–63
    Tillich and, 31–34
    weak messianic and, 56–58
    See "call," "deconstruction,"
        "theology, of perhaps,"
        "religion, as proto-religion,"
        "Tillich," the "unconditional"
Dostoevsky, Fyodor, on the Grand
    Inquisitor, 61–62
Eckhart, Meister, 12–13, 19, 69, 119
    see "mysticism"
Enlightenment, the, 27, 43, 48, 75, 97,
    98, 100, 127
event, see "deconstruction"
Freud, Sigmund, 43, 91
Gadamer, Hans-Georg, 54
God
    call of, 61, 78, 87–92, 106, 127
    death of, 32, 47, 51, 79–80,
        118–19
    existence of, 8, 11, 19–20, 70,
        73–74, 77, 78, 83, 95, 106–7,
        118, 119, 128
    folly of, 4–5, 43, 53, 58, 66, 78, 80,
        83, 103–4, 106–7, 112, 113,
        119, 123, 125
    incredulity about existence of,
        74–77
    insistence of, 34, 78, 83, 118, 127

137

ground of being and, 14–17, 66–69
hyperbeing of mystical theology
  and, 69–71
the perhaps and, 77–81
possibility of the impossible and, 37,
  45–46, 85–86
power of, 68, 113
sovereignty of, 31–32, 112
Supreme Being (*ens supremum*) and,
  1, 7–10, 12, 13, 19, 20, 32, 40,
  63, 68, 73–77, 97, 112–13
see "atheism," "event," "kingdom
  of God," "mysticism,"
  "theology," "unconditional,"
  "weakness"
hauntology, see "deconstruction"
Heidegger, Martin, 12, 33–34, 43, 54,
  66, 87–91, 115
Hegel, Georg F. W., 55, 68, 73, 78, 94
concept of *Vorstellung* in, 4, 65–66,
  96–105
Husserl, Edmund, 24
insistence
  distinguished from existence, 34,
    50, 92, 116, 118, 122, 126,128
  of the call, 34, 92, 122, 126–27
  of the event, 96, 115, 118–19
  of God, 78, 83, 106, 118–19, 128
  of the impossible, 116
  of justice, 56–57
  of the kingdom of God, 109,
    117–19
  of the unconditional, 34, 50, 78–81,
    96, 105, 115, 126–27
Jankelévitch, Vladimir, 62
Jesus (Yeshua), 3, 52, 58, 60–63, 71,
  94, 101, 107, 108, 115, 118,
  121, 122, 123
see "kingdom of God," "Son of
  Man"
Joachim of Fiore, 55
Kant, Immanuel, 27, 43, 75
Kierkegaard, Søren, 65, 96, 102–3
kingdom of God, 3, 17, 53, 58, 81, 92,
  107–9
coming of, 34, 52, 55–56, 59–60,
  71, 113–17

economy of rewards and, 25,
  123–24
event and, 115
folly of, 113–17, 119–25
fool's logic and, 108–9, 111–12,
  115–16
God and, 111, 116–19, 127–28
theopoetics of, 95, 106–7
weak force of, 62–63, 77, 109,
  111–12, 115
see "unconditional, hospitality;
  forgiveness"
Lacan, Jacques, 47–50, 91, 125
Levinas, Emmanuel, 66
Loisy, Abbé Alfred, 107
Lyotard, Jean-François, 73, 74, 76, 121
Malabou, Catherine, 24
Marion, Jean-Luc, 20
Martin, Dale, 60
Marx, Karl, 32–33, 43
mysticism, 12–13, 22, 55, 57, 66,
  69–71, 77, 80, 86, 88, 120
see "apophatic," "Eckhart, Meister"
Nietzsche, Friedrich, 5, 62, 80, 90, 123
Paul, Saint
  body of Christ and, 34
  folly of God and, 4, 58–61, 66,
    103, 111, 120
  *kenosis* and, 55
  logic of the cross and, 4, 95, 99
  return of Jesus and, 108
  weakness of God and, 2, 4, 58–61,
    66, 78, 108, 12
pantheism vs. panentheism, 15, 68, 78
psychoanalysis, 48–49, 73
  see "Lacan"
religion
  confessional form of, 2, 39, 49–50,
    75–76, 88, 96, 112, 120, 122,
    124
  deconstructibility of, 24, 25, 28, 31,
    32, 39–40
  Hegel on, 96–102, 104
  Marx on, 32–33
  of the future, 51–52
  proto-religion and, 2, 35–37, 50–
    52, 56, 86, 104–5

psychoanalysis and, 47–50, 73
theological virtues and, 36–37
two examples of proto-religion and, 40–47
versus secular, 27
without religion, 2, 37, 41, 50
see "Hegel, concept of *Vorstellung*," "unconditional"
Rorty, Richard, 54
Schelling, F. W., 68, 96, 102
Son of Man, coming of, 119–25
Socrates, 13, 104
theology
classical sense of, 1–2, 94–95
distinguished from theopoetics, 3, 93–96, 119
interest in God of, 1–2, 19
of culture, 40, 51, 56
of "perhaps, " 77–81
of the unconditional, 2–3, 4–5, 22, 39, 50–52, 65, 70, 88–89, 103, 118, 124, 126
strong form of, 1–2, 10, 13
weak (radical) form of, 1–2, 10, 53, 56, 59–60, 65, 66–67, 69, 77, 80, 92, 93, 95, 103, 105–6, 124
see "event," "unconditional," "theopoetics"
theopoetics, 3, 45, 85–86, 128
defined, 93–96, 105–6
Hegel and, 96–102, 104
of the kingdom of God, 17, 107–19
see "theology, distinguished from theopoetics"
Tillich, Paul,
atheism of, 8–15, 23, 43, 66, 79, 96, 106
courage to be and, 43, 53
deconstruction and, 21–35
father of radical theology, 96

ground of being and, 14–17, 41, 66–69, 71, 86, 88, 101, 104
the Protestant Principle and the Jewish Principle and, 31–34, 54, 84, 89, 117, 126
the symbolic and, 102–3
theology of culture and, 40, 51, 56
ultimate concern and, 37
see "Aquinas," "theology," the "unconditional"
Titanic, the sinking of, 41–43
unconditional, the, 4–5, 19
coming Son of Man and, 121–26
Derrida and, 29–34, 49–52 56–58, 76–77, 91–92
God and, 13–14, 19–21, 49–50, 77–81, 103–4
theology of perhaps and, 77–81
Tillich and, 13–17, 19–21, 48, 76–77, 79, 192
weak force and, 56–58, 112–14
See "call," "religion, as proto-religion," "theology, of the unconditional"
Vattimo, Gianni, 53–56
weakness
courage, and 53
economy of, 5–6, 60–61, 112, 123–27
ground of being and, 66–69
kingdom of God and, 63
mystical theology and, 69–71
of God, 1–4, 32, 53, 55, 58–64, 66, 108–9, 119, 122, 127
of kingdom of God, 112–13
weak thought, 53–56
weak Messianic force, 56–58
See "theology, weak form of"
Žižek, Slavoj, 49

# About the Author

**John D. Caputo** (Ph.D., Bryn Mawr College) is the Watson Professor of Religion Emeritus at Syracuse University and the Cook Professor of Philosophy Emeritus at Villanova University. A hybrid philosopher/theologian who works in the area of radical theology, Caputo is the author of many books, including *The Insistence of God* (2013), *The Weakness of God* (2006), winner of the American Academy of Religion award for excellence in constructive theology, *Hoping Against Hope* (2015), and the *The Folly of God* (2015).